Manage Your Student Finances Now!

Keith Houghton

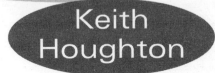

**Easy ways
to balance your
budget at university
and college**

Vermilion
LONDON

For Matthew xx

For all the lost weekends and evenings he had to put up with!

3 5 7 9 10 8 6 4 2

First published in the United Kingdom in 2003
by Vermilion, an imprint of Ebury Press
Random House UK Ltd.
Random House
20 Vauxhall Bridge Road
London SW1V 2SA

Random House Australia (Pty) Limited
20 Alfred Street, Milsons Point, Sydney,
New South Wales 2061, Australia

Random House New Zealand Limited
18 Poland Road, Glenfield,
Auckland 10, New Zealand

Random House (Pty) Limited
Endulini, 5A Jubilee Road, Parktown 2193, South Africa

Random House UK Limited Reg. No. 954009
www.randomhouse.co.uk
Papers used by Vermilion are natural, recyclable products made from wood grown in
sustainable forests.

A CIP catalogue record is available for this book from the British Library.

ISBN: 0091891612

Printed and bound in Great Britain by
Bookmarque Ltd, Croydon, Surrey

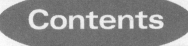
Contents

Part 2 **Banking and Credit**

Part 3 **Where Does All
the Money Go?**

Part 4 Juggling Your
            (Limited) Finances

Part 5   After the Course

Introduction

Going to university and moving away from home for the first time is quite a daunting prospect. There are so many courses and universities to choose from and so many things to consider – what the place is like, whether you really want to do that course, what the job prospects will be when you finish – amongst other things. Leaving the 'safety' of the family home, friends and familiar places is scary enough without also having to consider the issue of money. Recent estimates put the cost of living as a student somewhere in the region of £6,000–£7,000 per year. Add to that a student loan which does not cover the full amount of those costs and you will soon see that there could be trouble ahead. That is where this book can help! A wise academic once said that a student who successfully manages to budget through their first year of university should be credited with a first-year module in budgeting and money management. Well, if such a module actually existed, this would surely be the recommended textbook!

As you read on, you will find information about the sources of income you can get. I have been a student money adviser for some years now and it is still surprising just how many students are unaware of the sources of funding open to them. If you are going to survive even the first year of your course, you need to have enough money to get through, so it is essential to know how and when to apply for it. For example, did you know that for a course starting in September, you need to make your initial application for student support by mid-March, six months beforehand? Once you have the money you need to make sure it lasts, so you will find information on how to draw up a budget and keep your spending in check.

But financial survival is not just about income. It is also about effectively managing that income and your expenditure to prevent a crisis from happening. For the first and possibly only time in your life, you may be faced with money coming in just three times a year, once per term. That money needs to last so careful budgeting is vital to your survival. If you draw up a budget and stick to it then you should get much more from your student experience. If you are not constantly worrying about your finances, you are likely to fare better academically and be less stressed. At the back of this book you will find a blank budget planner that you can use to plan your budget. Make a realistic budget and stick to it and you should be OK. Of course, unplanned emergencies always occur, bills start piling up and you get into debt. Don't panic! You will find strategies for dealing with debt in this book, too.

Of course, this book cannot be a substitute for detailed individual advice and it has not been possible to cover every eventuality or scenario. To do that would make the book very long and largely irrelevant to you. Think of it, therefore, as a set of pointers and places to start. I am not going to 'nanny' you along the way and say you must do this or you must not do that; I will merely point out useful ideas you might like to consider. Most universities and colleges and/or their students' unions, guilds or associations have trained money advisers who are there to help. Don't be frightened to ask for help from them – remember it is what they are there for. Some universities also run money management and budgeting workshops for new students. These are well worth going to, even if you think you know how to draw up a budget and stick to it.

Above all, I hope that by using this book as a regular resource, you will worry less about money and finances and be able to get on with what you are at university for in the first place – drink! Ooops, I meant to say study. . .

Good luck with your studies!

Keith Houghton
Surbiton, March 2003

Getting the Money In

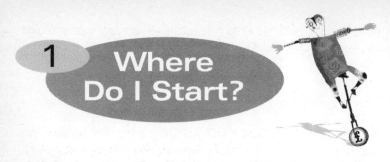

1 Where Do I Start?

Before you can compile a budget, you need to make sure you know what your income is. For most people, this is simply a case of working out how much their take-home pay will be at the end of each month, or the amount of benefit they will receive. For students in higher education it is more complicated than that. The days when all students received a maintenance grant are long gone and grants have, by and large, been replaced by student loans. Thanks to devolution, there are now also various systems in place in different parts of the UK. So before you can begin to budget and manage your finances effectively, you need to know what sources of income you can access and how and when to apply for them. The rest of this section looks at that in more detail. The money you can get will depend on where you live at the moment and the type of course you will be studying, as shown in the chart.

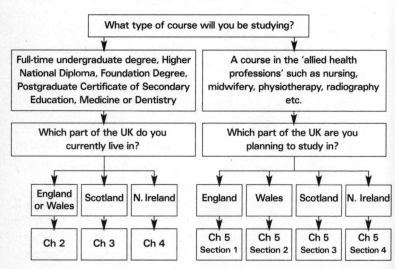

Read this chapter then turn to the section relevant to you as indicated by the chart. NB Part-time and overseas students should turn to Chapter 7.

Terminology

The student support system includes some terms and phrases you may have not have heard before. Before going into any detail about what you might get, it is worth briefly explaining what some of those terms mean. . .

Local Education Authority The local authority responsible for handling your application for student support. In England and Wales, this might be your local council if you live in a 'unitary' authority. If you live in a 'unitary' authority, one council is responsible for provision of education and student support services and collection of Council Tax. Examples of unitary authorities include Southampton, Reading and Slough. In other cases a local district or borough council will collect Council Tax but a county council will be responsible for education and student support. For example, if you live in Epsom, you pay Council Tax to Epsom and Ewell Council but Surrey County Council are responsible for student support. This does not apply to London Boroughs which are, in effect, also unitary authorities. A full list of student support contacts can be found in Appendix A. Otherwise it will be your county or borough council. In Scotland, all student support applications are handled by the Student Awards Agency for Scotland in Edinburgh, and in Northern Ireland by the Education and Library Boards.

Student Loan A loan from the Government towards your living costs whilst you are studying. The student loan is repaid after graduation.

Tuition Fees Money you pay to your university or college for your course. Under current rules, students contribute around 25% of the cost of tuition with the rest coming from public funds. Students from countries outside the European Union will often have to pay much higher fees, sometimes up to £8,000 per year. Scottish and EU students who study in Scotland do not have to pay tuition fees.

Grant for Tuition Fees A grant towards the cost of tuition fees – not everyone has to pay the full amount. The latest Government estimate is that approximately 40% of students will not have to pay any tuition fees at all, 30% will have to pay a proportion and 30% will have to pay the full amount.

Dependants' Allowances Additional allowances paid to students with children or other dependants. These are paid as grants and do not have to be repaid.

Disabled Students' Allowances Additional allowances paid to some disabled students. These allowances do not depend on income and do not have to be repaid.

NHS Bursaries Students on nursing, midwifery and other health-profession courses (excluding medicine and dentistry) receive a different package of support and usually qualify for bursaries from the National Health Service.

Eligibility

Now you know which chapter will be relevant to you, you first need to find out if you are eligible for funding. There are common rules across the UK with some variations and exceptions. You need to meet ALL the conditions to be eligible for student support funding.

Residency

This is probably the most complex rule to understand. To meet the criteria you must have been 'ordinarily resident' in the UK, Channel Islands or Isle of Man for at least three years on the 'relevant date'. The 'relevant date' is taken to be 1 September if you start your course between September and December (1 August for courses in Scotland where the academic year starts earlier). The rules say that you must have been living there as part of your 'ordinary life'. If you came to the UK during that time principally for the purposes of education, you will not be eligible and therefore unable to apply for any support at all. If you are not a United Kingdom national, you must also have 'settled status' on the relevant date. Broadly speaking, this means there must be no restriction on your stay for an immigration reason.

EXAMPLES

Pauline came to the UK in 2000 to do her A levels. She is originally from Nigeria. She is not eligible for student support funding as her main purpose in the UK for at least two of those three years was for education.

Olukayode is from Ghana and was granted Indefinite Leave to Remain in the UK in 2001. He had been in the UK since 1997. As there is no restriction on his stay (his leave does not run out on a certain date), he is eligible for student support funding.

The main exceptions to these rules are:

- Students who have been living temporarily in another European Economic Area country because their parents were employed in that country. (The EEA is made up of the European Union plus Iceland, Norway and Liechtenstein.)
- Nationals and spouses of nationals from other EEA countries who have 'migrant worker' status or whose parents are or have been migrant workers in the UK.
- People (and their families) who have been recognised as refugees by the British Government.
- People (and their families) who have been granted 'Exceptional Leave to Remain' or 'Exceptional Leave to Enter' the UK as the result of a failed asylum application.

If you think you might be in one of these groups, speak to your relevant authority for more information as the rules are very complex. You can find details of your relevant authority in Chapters 2–5, depending on where you currently live or, in the case of healthcare-profession students, where you will be studying.

In addition to all the above, to qualify for certain supplementary grants made by the devolved assemblies or Scottish Parliament, you must also be 'ordinarily resident' in that particular country of the UK on your 'relevant date'.

European Union Students

Students from EU countries (excluding the UK) who have been 'ordinarily resident' in the UK for three years prior to the start of the course must apply to the Home Office for 'settled status' before the 'relevant date'. This means that, although you will have a right of abode in the UK, you must make an application for Indefinite Leave to Remain in order to qualify for support towards tuition fees and living costs.

If you do not have 'settled status' you might still be able to apply for support towards your tuition fees if:

- You are an EU national, or child or stepchild of an EU national; and
- You have been ordinarily resident in an EU member state, or another EEA country, for at least three years prior to the start of your course; and
- You will be taking a full-time course.

At the time of writing, there were plans for the enlargement of the European Union to 25 countries from the present 15. It is likely that nationals of the additional countries will be able to apply for support towards their tuition fees from the next academic year after the date on which their home country becomes a member of the European Union. If this applies to you, check with your relevant authority for further information.

Course Eligibility

To be eligible for funding, your course must be an 'eligible course' and you must be studying at a university or college that receives public funds. For students studying full-time courses, this includes:

- Full-time first degree courses at universities in the UK, leading to awards such as BA, BSc or LLB. For students from Scotland and Northern Ireland, courses at Trinity College, Dublin, and the National University of Ireland (University College Dublin, University College Cork and University College Galway) are also eligible courses.
- Higher National Diplomas (HND).
- Foundation Degrees.

- Certificate or Diploma of Higher Education (CertHE and DipHE courses).
- Foundation courses where the entry requirements are the same as for the degree but only if you enrol for the whole course (i.e. foundation plus degree) and the university treats the foundation course as a necessary part of the degree.
- Sandwich courses, where your course involves periods of practical work experience and you study full-time.

Most universities and colleges in the UK receive public funds. Some private colleges and the University of Buckingham, the UK's main private university, have courses that are 'specifically designated'. This means that although the course is taught at a private institution, it receives some public funding, and students on those courses can receive student support funding. The rules on this, as with most other elements of student support, are complicated, so seek advice from your LEA/ELB/SAAS if you are considering a course at a private university or college.

EXAMPLES

June will be starting a BSc in Physics in September. Her course is an eligible course.

Debbie will be starting an AVCE course in September. Because this is a 'school level' course, it is not eligible for student support.

Cameron will be starting a National Certificate in IT course in September. This is a course of further education and is not eligible for student support.

Sinead will enrol on a Foundation Degree in Aircraft Engineering in February. This is an 'eligible course' so she can apply for student support.

The main sort of course that is not eligible for student support is the Foundation Course in Art and Design offered by many universities and colleges of art and design. In most cases, this course does not necessarily form an integral part of a degree course and can be studied without progressing to a degree in art and design. If you are aged under 19 when you start the course, which usually lasts for one year, and you will be studying in England, your tuition fees should be paid by the Learning and Skills Council. In addition, you may be able to apply to your university or college for assistance from the Access to Learning Fund or Learner Support Fund, depending on your university or college. Foundation art and design students are not eligible to apply for student loans.

Part-time Courses

Part-time degree courses attract a different package of student support. However, the general eligibility requirements are broadly the same as those for full-time courses.

Your Age

There is no age restriction on grants for tuition fees. You are therefore eligible to apply for these regardless of your age. Nor is there any age restriction on Dependants' Allowances, if you have dependent children or adults, or are on Disabled Students' Allowances.

To qualify for a student loan, you must be aged under 50. However, if you are aged between 50 and 54 at the start of the course and can show that you intend to go back to work once you have completed your course, you will also be eligible. If you do not plan to go back to work, or are aged over 55, you will not be eligible for a student loan at all, but may be able to apply for assistance with tuition fees and other supplementary grants. There are no age restrictions on eligibility for NHS bursaries.

Previous Study

There are complicated rules on how previous study may affect your entitlement to student support funding, although there is currently no restriction on previous study for NHS bursaries. As a general rule, if you have had support from 'public funds' before, you will not be entitled to any assistance with tuition fees. This support can include old-style grants if you were studying before 1998, any discretionary award for a higher-education course, awards from other Government departments including NHS bursaries, or public support for tuition fees. Even if you did not have to make a personal contribution to tuition fees, remember that the Government will have paid about 75% of the actual cost of tuition if you have already studied a higher-education course.

EXAMPLES

Polly has just finished her A2 levels and will be going to university in September. As she has never had support from public funds for a higher-education course before, she is eligible for support towards her tuition fees.

Narinder did a nursing course a few years ago and received an NHS bursary. She is now going back to university to study pharmaceutical science. As she has had support from public funds already, she is not eligible for support towards her tuition fees.

Soo-Yin attended a private music college where she did her HND. She is now in the first year of a performing arts degree. Her college received money from public funds towards her tuition fees so she is not eligible for support towards her tuition fees for her degree course.

As mentioned above, the rules are very complicated and it is not possible to cover all possible scenarios in this book. Your LEA/ELB/SAAS can give you more information on eligibility for assistance with tuition fees if you have studied at higher education level already.

Previous study will not affect your entitlement to a student loan or to any additional grants to which you might be entitled. However, if you are due to be repaying a student loan you took out whilst studying and you are in arrears or have defaulted on the repayments, you will not be able to get any further support until those arrears or the default are cleared. This means that any public support to tuition fees, additional grants and student loan payments will not be paid until the arrears are cleared. This does cause a problem for some students. If you find yourself in this situation, you should contact your student services department as they may be able to offer a short-term loan from their Access to Learning, Hardship, Financial Contingency or Support Funds to help you clear the arrears. You will need to pay this money back as soon as you receive your student loan payment.

What you need to do and when – applying for funding

If you will be starting your course in September:

In February	Contact your LEA, ELB or SAAS for an application form.
	Fill in the form and send it back! If you live in England, Wales or Northern Ireland your LEA or ELB will send you a financial form.
In April	Students from England, Wales and Northern Ireland need to fill in the financial form.
In May	Students from Scotland need to send their application form back to SAAS to make sure they receive the first payment in time for the start of term!
During the summer	If you can, work as much as possible and save up! The money will come in very useful at the start of term (remember you will probably also have to pay a deposit for your accommodation).
	Make sure you have opened a bank account and that the Student Loans Company know your bank details. If you don't tell them, they can't pay you!
One month before your course starts	Students from England, Wales and Northern Ireland must send the Loan Request Form to the Student Loans Company to make sure they receive their first payment at the start of term!

N.B. This information does not apply to students who live in 'pilot' LEAs in England (see Chapter 2) or to healthcare students (see Chapter 5).

Remember, in order for you to be eligible to receive funding for your study, you must fulfil *all* the eligibility requirements, that is:

- Residency, AND
- Course eligibility, AND
- Age, AND
- Previous study, AND
- No arrears or default on a pre-existing student loan

So far, we have looked only at entitlement to support for 'home' UK students. Information on funding for other students – international, European Union and 'islands' (Channel Islands and Isle of Man) – can be found in Chapter 7. If you are a 'home' student, turn now to the relevant chapter to see exactly what you can get so you can start thinking about planning your budget.

2 Show Me the Money! (Part One)

Statutory Funding for Students from England and Wales

What Might You Get?

Having established that you are eligible for student support funding, you now need to know what you can apply for. Thankfully, from September 2003 the system has been simplified, reducing the number of grants and other statutory sources and simplifying application processes.

Summary of What is Available

- Student loan of up to £4,930 (at 2003/04 rates), depending on where you study and on your, your parents' or partner's income
- Assistance with tuition fees of up to £1,125 (at 2003/04 rates), depending on your, your parents' or partner's income
- Additional help if you have a disability, known as a 'Disabled Students' Allowance'
- Additional help if you have an adult dependant
- Additional help if you have dependent children
- Bursary of up to £3,400 for students from England on social work degree courses

- Welsh students from low-income families may also qualify for an Assembly Learning Grant
- English students from low-income families may also qualify for an Opportunity Bursary (if starting in September 2003) or an HE Grant (if starting in September 2004)

Not all students will qualify for all the above funding as certain grants are only available to particular groups of students. However, all students can apply for the following funding.

Grants for Tuition Fees

First, let's clear one thing up. In 2003/04 and 2004/05 you will *not* have to pay any top-up or differential fees. This does not come into force until September 2006 so if you are starting a three-year course in September 2003, they will not apply to you. Having established that, we can now look at what you might have to pay. The maximum fee that can be charged for 'Home' students on a full-time course in 2003/04 is £1,125. Tuition fees are paid for each year of study and, under current rules, increase annually in line with inflation. You may find you are entitled to some help from your Local Education Authority towards paying the tuition fees. Once your LEA has confirmed that you are eligible to receive student support, they will send you a form (called a Form HE2) that asks questions about your, your parents' or your partner's income. They need this information so they can undertake an income assessment, more commonly known as a means test. In 2003, some LEAs in England are taking part in a pilot scheme that will be looking at other methods for students to apply for support. Your LEA will tell you if they are using the new procedure, and there is a list in the section on student loans, but the information here about means-testing is still relevant to you.

From the information on your form and the documents sent with it, which can include P60s and/or payslips, your LEA will work out whether or not you (or your parents or partner) have to make a contribution towards tuition fees. There are complex rules on how the contributions work, the main points of which are outlined in the table below.

Contributions – How They Work (2003/04 rates shown)	
If you are assessed as dependent on your parents	For residual income below £20,970, NO CONTRIBUTION. For a residual income of £20,970, a contribution of £45. Contribution increases by £1 for each £9.50 of additional residual income.
If you have a partner	For residual income below £18,040, NO CONTRIBUTION. For a residual income of £18,040, a contribution of £45. Contribution increases by £1 for each £8 of additional residual income.
If you are an independent student	The first £7,500 of certain income is ignored, as are certain allowances for income such as sponsorship, part-time work during your course and certain benefits. If income is above this level, you are expected to make a contribution, pound for pound.

As you can see from the table, the rules are very complicated! You are probably wondering what residual income actually means. Contrary to popular belief, it is not income minus tax and National Insurance payments. Broadly speaking, it refers to gross income with deductions made for pension payments that qualify for tax relief, other adult dependants, a parent who is also a student and certain other deductions that will only apply to a very small number of people – your LEA can give you more information. In the case of parents or partners, the LEA will look at income from the previous tax year – 2003/04 for students starting courses in September 2004. If the income is likely to be significantly lower in the year you will be studying, you can ask your LEA to look again at your application, taking into account the new information. If you are classed as an independent student, you will need to estimate your income for the year you will be studying.

You become liable to pay the maximum fee of £1,125 in the following cases:

- Your parents' residual income is £31,230; or
- Your partner's residual income is £26,680; or
- If you are classed as an independent student, your income during the year you will be studying is greater than £7,500 by £1,125 or more; or
- You decide not to apply for means-tested support

(Remember, these are 2003/04 rates so if you are starting your course after September 2003 they will probably be increased in line with inflation.)

Many students do not realise that once their eligibility has been confirmed, they need to provide further income details in order to have their fee liability assessed. There are, as ever, some exceptions to these rules – especially if you have a brother or sister who is also at university, or if there are other children for whom your parents are responsible. If this applies to you, ask your LEA for more information.

The Government expects partners or parents who are assessed as liable to make a contribution to actually make it. However, there is no legal compulsion on them to pay up, which leaves some students with reduced amounts of loans and bills from their universities for tuition fees. If this happens to you, speak to a student adviser or welfare officer at your university or students' union.

How Do I Apply?

Apply to your LEA – the same form is used for applying for a grant for fees, a student loan and any additional grants (except Disabled Students' Allowances).

How is it Paid?

If you have to pay all or some of the tuition fees yourself, your university will tell you how and when to pay.

If your LEA is paying some or all of the tuition fees on your behalf, they will instruct the Student Loans Company (SLC) to pay the fees direct to your university.

EXAMPLE

Sanjeev's LEA has advised him that a parental contribution of £458 is due.
This means that the LEA will instruct the SLC to pay £667 of his tuition fees direct to the university.
Sanjeev's parents are responsible for paying the remaining £458 by whatever method the university requires.

SEE ALSO
Chapter 10 – bills
Chapter 13 – dealing with debt

Student Loans

The student loan has two elements – a non-means-tested element and a means-tested element. This means that, even if your parents are very well off, provided you meet the eligibility criteria outlined in Chapter 1, you can qualify for the non-means-tested element of the loan. Maximum student loan rates for students from England and Wales in 2003/04 are (final-year figures are in brackets):

	Non Means Tested (75%)	Means Tested (25%)	Total
London	£3,695 (£3,205)	£1,235 (£1,070)	£4,930 (£4,275)
Outside London	£3,000 (£2,605)	£1,000 (£865)	£4,000 (£3,470)
Living with parents	£2,375 (£2,070)	£790 (£695)	£3,165 (£2,765)

If you study at a campus of a university in London and do not live with your parents whilst studying, you will qualify for the London rate of loan. If you study outside London and do not live with your parents, you will qualify for the Outside London rate of loan (usually referred to as the 'Elsewhere' rate). If you live with your parents, you will qualify for the Parental Home rate of loan, regardless of where you study.

EXAMPLES

Susan will be going to the University of Nottingham and will live in halls of residence. She will qualify for the 'Elsewhere' rate of student loan.

Gary will be studying at the University of Westminster and live with his parents whilst studying. Even though his university is in London, he will qualify for the 'Parental Home' rate of loan.

Hema lives in rented accommodation and studies at the London School of Economics. She qualifies for the 'London' rate of loan.

If you receive the means-tested loan and you have to attend your course for more than 30 weeks, not including vacations, you may receive an extra amount of loan as follows:

- £92 per week if you get the London rate of loan
- £71 per week if you get the Elsewhere rate of loan
- £48 per week if you get the Parental Home rate of loan

You do not need to make a separate application for the extra weeks' loan as it should be added automatically to your loan entitlement by your LEA from the information they have about courses at your particular university.

EXAMPLE

Martina gets the London rate of loan and she has to attend her course for 35 weeks of the year. If she gets the full means-tested loan, she is therefore entitled to:

London rate loan	£4,930
Extra weeks (5)	£460
Full loan entitlement	£5,390

The means-test used for student loans is the same as for tuition fees. You already know that if, for example, your parents' income is £31,230 then they are assessed as liable to pay the full tuition fee, but what if their income is above this level? The answer is that the means-tested loan, including any extra weeks' loan, starts to be reduced. If you are assessed on the basis of your partner's income, this threshold is £26,680.

E X A M P L E

Andrew is going to a university outside London and will be living in halls of residence. His course has three extra weeks. His parents have a residual income of £38,500. Before the means test, Andrew's maximum loan entitlement would be as follows:

Non-means-tested loan (Elsewhere rate)	£3,000
Means-tested loan (Elsewhere rate)	£1,000
Extra weeks' loan (3 weeks @ £71 each)	£213
Total	£4,213

Since Andrew's parents have an income of £38,500, which is above £31,230, his means-tested loan is reduced by £765. His total loan entitlement is therefore £3,448.

E X A M P L E

Caroline will be studying at a university in London and living at home with her husband who has a residual income of £24,000.

Caroline qualifies for the London rate loan and, because her husband earns less than £26,680, she will get the full means-tested loan of £4,930.

(However, her husband will be assessed as having to make a contribution towards Caroline's tuition fees.)

E X A M P L E

Stuart will be going to a university outside London and living in halls of residence. If he were entitled to the maximum means-tested loan, he would get £4,000. However, his parents' residual income is £68,000.

This means that their assessed contribution is £3,870. The first £1,125 of this contribution is towards tuition fees. His loan will be reduced by £1,000 so that he receives the non-means-tested element of £3,000. This is the absolute minimum he can get, even though the assessed parental contribution is greater.

How Do I Apply for the Loan?

1. Unless you are in a pilot area (City of Birmingham, Durham, East Sussex, Hampshire, Nottinghamshire, London Borough of Waltham Forest or Wiltshire) you first apply to your LEA for an eligibility assessment. If you live in a pilot area, your LEA will tell you how to apply for the loan.
2. Once the LEA has decided that you are eligible for support, they will send you a financial assessment form which you complete and send back. They will then work out whether any contribution to either fees or the student loan is due.
3. The LEA sends you a form called a 'Financial Assessment'. You will be sent three copies – one for you to keep and one to give to the university. Fill in the back of the third copy as this is the Loan Request Form, and send it to SLC at least one month before you are due to start your course, if this is possible.

This applies to 'new' students. If you are going into the second or subsequent year of study and have applied for support previously you will not need to complete another eligibility assessment.

When Should I Apply?

Do not wait until you have final exam results and know which university you are going to. The application process can take several weeks or months, particularly in LEAs where there are lots of students. For example, if you are starting your course in September, your eligibility assessment form should be sent to your LEA by the middle of the preceding March at the latest, and the financial assessment form by mid-June at the latest in order to guarantee payment of the loan at the start of the autumn term.

How is it Paid?

The loan is usually paid in three instalments if you apply to the SLC in the first term of the academic year; in two instalments if you apply in the second term and in one lump sum if you apply in the third term. Second and third instalments are always paid by BACS transfer directly into your bank account. In September 2003, most students will receive their first instalment by BACS and some by cheque. It is expected that all students will receive first instalments by BACS in September 2004.

Quick Guide – Tuition Fees and Student Loans

- Apply to your LEA from January 2003 (January 2004 if you are starting your course in September 2004)
- Complete both the eligibility and income assessment forms to see if you have to pay any tuition fees or make a contribution to your living costs
- Apply to SLC for the loan as early as you can
- Open a bank account before going to university so it is ready to receive your first student loan payment

SEE ALSO
Chapter 8 – bank accounts
Chapter 15 – repaying your loan

Additional Grants

So far in this chapter, we have looked at funding available to all full-time students from England and Wales. Whilst that covers funding for the majority of students who will be going to university, there are a number of additional grants available to some groups of students.

Disabled Students' Allowances

Disabled Students' Allowances, or DSAs, are grants paid by the LEA to help with extra costs you incur whilst studying as a result of a disability. You can apply for a DSA at any time before or during your course. It is made up of a number of different elements.

Specialist Equipment Allowance. The amount you get depends on the level of need as agreed with the LEA. It is a one-off payment for the duration of the course that can pay for items such as laptop computers, voice-recognition software or any other specialist equipment you need in order to take part in your course. The maximum that the LEA will pay in 2003/04 is £4,460 for the duration of the course.

> **EXAMPLE**
>
> Ben has been diagnosed as dyslexic. He needs a laptop computer, costing £1,400, and special voice-recognition software, costing £250. The LEA will either purchase the equipment through their suppliers on Ben's behalf, or ask Ben to buy it and reimburse him on production of receipts. (Different LEAs have different procedures.)

Non-medical Helpers' Allowance can help with the cost of paying for non-medical support. This can include sign-language interpreters, note-takers etc. Once again, the amount you receive depends on your assessed level of need. The non-medical helpers' allowance is paid each year and the maximum for 2003/04 is £11,280.

> **EXAMPLE**
>
> Katrina is deaf and needs the help of a sign-language interpreter and a note-taker in order to be able to attend classes. The total cost of this over the year is £15,000. However, her DSA can only cover £11,280 of this cost, leaving a shortfall of £3,720. Katrina can apply to her university's Access to Learning, Hardship or Financial Contingency Fund to help meet this shortfall.

General Disabled Students' Allowance is also available for general costs incurred as a result of a disability. In 2003/04, the maximum is £1,490. The General DSA can be paid for each year of the course.

Additional Travel Costs. If your travel costs are higher as a result of your disability, you can claim for the additional costs, over and above the amount of everyday travel costs.

> **EXAMPLE**
>
> Florence is disabled and unable to use public transport to get to her place of study. Her only other option is to take a taxi each way. Travel by bus would normally cost her £10 per week. Travel by taxi costs £60 per week. Her LEA has agreed to pay the additional £50 per week direct to the taxi company on Florence's behalf.

What Do I Need to Prove?

This will depend on the nature of the disability. However, in most cases you will need to provide your LEA with medical evidence such as a letter from your GP or hospital consultant. If you are dyslexic, you will need to provide a report from an educational psychologist that has been prepared within the last two years. This can be a problem as these reports are quite expensive to obtain, usually between £200 and £300. Most universities now have a disability adviser or dyslexia support service, sometimes called learning support. If you think you might be dyslexic, it could be worth contacting them first and they may be able to offer an initial screening to see if you really need an appointment with an educational psychologist. If they think you might be dyslexic they will give you contact details for educational psychologists – some universities have links with local psychologists who may provide the assessments at a special rate for students, so it is always worth asking. If you find that you cannot afford the cost of the test, contact your university student services department to see if you can apply for help from the Hardship Fund towards the cost of the assessment.

In order to assess the level of support required, the LEA may ask you to make an appointment with a Needs Assessor, usually based at an ACCESS centre. They will discuss your needs with you and may ask you to undertake some tests. They then make a report to your LEA and your LEA decides on the level of additional financial support they will pay.

Whom Do I Apply to?

You apply to your LEA using a special Disabled Students' Allowance application form. Any amount you receive is not dependent on your, your parents' or your partner's income. It is based solely on the additional needs you have as a result of the disability.

How is it Paid?

Specialist Equipment Allowances may be paid directly to the supplier of the equipment, or direct to you on production of receipts. Procedures vary among LEAs so your LEA will tell you what arrangements they have in place.

Non-medical Helpers' Allowances may be paid direct to the organisation supplying the assistance or direct to you – again, procedures vary among LEAs.

General DSA will be paid to you as a cheque to collect from your university at the beginning of each term.

Travel Costs – arrangements vary so ask your LEA.

Further Help and Advice

- The Disability Adviser at your university
- Most LEAs have a specific person responsible for DSAs
- SKILL – The National Bureau for Students with Disabilities. Their contact details can be found in Appendix B.
- Department for Education and Skills booklet *Bridging the Gap,* available from your LEA or from the DfES Student Support Information Line on Freephone 0800 731 9133 or textphone 0800 328 8988. The booklet is also available online at www.dfes.gov.uk/studentsupport/formsandguides/index.shtml

Care Leavers' Grant

The Care Leavers' Grant is a non-repayable grant that can be paid to some students who were in care for at least three months following their 16th birthday and are aged under 21 on starting their courses. It is intended to cover the costs of accommodation during the long summer vacation and is worth up to £100 per week, depending on the actual cost of the accommodation. However, the Children (Leaving Care) Act 2000 is now in force so if you were aged 16 or 17 on 1 October 2001 and in care on that date or afterwards, you may be entitled to additional support from Social Services rather than through the Care Leavers' Grant. This additional support is available for all the vacations whilst you are at university. Your social worker, if you have one, or your personal adviser will be able to give you more information.

How Do I Apply?

To your LEA.

How is it Paid?

Care Leavers' Grant is paid for the long summer vacation only. It will be paid direct to you by your LEA or to your landlord if you agree to the LEA paying it in this way.

Grants for Adult Dependants

If you have an adult who is financially dependent on you, whether it is your husband, wife, partner or another adult relative, you may qualify for an Adult Dependants' Grant. It is means-tested and the amount you actually receive will depend on your income and the income of the adults who are dependent on you. For 2003/04, the maximum Adult Dependants' Grant is £2,280.

How Do I Apply?

When you fill in your income assessment form, you will be asked for details of any dependants you have. There is no special extra form to fill in.

How is it Paid?

The Adult Dependants' Grant will usually be paid in three instalments, along with payments of your student loan.

Parents' Learning Allowance

This is a new grant being introduced from September 2003, replacing Dependants Additions and Travel Books and Equipment Grants, previously administered by LEAs, and Access Bursaries, previously administered by universities. They are provided to help with additional course-related costs incurred by student parents. The allowance is means-tested so the amount you get will depend on your income and that of your dependants. The LEA will look at the income of the family as a whole, including your husband, wife or partner, if you have one. If your children have any income of their own, for example from a trust fund, the LEA will take this into account when working out your entitlement. The income thresholds are quite low and you will only receive the maximum grant of £1,300 per year (2003/04 rates) if the total family income is below the levels listed below:

- £5,000 if you are a lone parent with two or more children
- £4,000 if you are a lone parent with one child; or if you are in a couple and have two or more children
- £3,000 if you are in a couple with one child

If the total family income is above these amounts, the Parents' Learning Allowance you can receive is reduced on a pound-for-pound basis down to a minimum grant of £50.

EXAMPLE

Esther is a single parent with two children. The family has no other income so Esther will receive the full Parents' Learning Allowance of £1,300.

EXAMPLE

Patrick and Sofia have two children. Patrick is a full-time student and Sofia works, earning £4,500 per year. As Sofia's income is above the threshold of £4,000 for a couple with two or more children, Patrick's Parents' Learning Allowance is reduced by £1 for every £1 that Sofia earns above the threshold. Patrick should therefore receive a Parents' Learning Allowance of £800.

How Do I Apply?

When you fill in your income assessment form, you will be asked for details of any dependants you have. There is no special extra form to fill in.

How is it Paid?

The Parents' Learning Allowance will usually be paid in three instalments, along with payments of your student loan.

Childcare Grants

Childcare Grants are available to help students who have dependant children with the cost of certain types of childcare. Qualifying childcare includes private day nurseries, local-authority nurseries, registered childminders and out-of-hours school clubs. If you use informal childcare, for example if your children are looked after by a neighbour or friend, you will not qualify for a Childcare Grant.

Childcare Grant Rates

1 child	Up to £114.75 per week (85% of £135 per week)
2 or more children	Up to £170.00 per week (85% of £200 per week)

The Childcare Grant can cover up to 85% of the actual costs of your registered childcare, even during the long summer vacation if you need to pay to keep a place open for your child. However, the amount the grant can cover is capped to a maximum of £135 per week if you have one child, or £200 per week if you have two or more children. If you pay less than £135 or £200 per week, your Childcare Grant will cover 85% of the amount you actually pay.

EXAMPLES

Gloria has two children and both attend nursery. The fees are £80 per week for each child, meaning that Gloria pays £160 per week.
Gloria's Childcare Grant would therefore be £136 per week, or 85% of £160.

Tony has one child attending a local private nursery at a cost of £150 per week.
As the weekly charge exceeds the maximum the Childcare Grant can cover, Tony's Childcare Grant will be £114.75 per week, or 85% of £135. Tony will need to meet the shortfall himself (though he could apply for extra help from the university's Hardship Fund).

The Childcare Grant is means-tested in the same way as the Parents' Learning Allowance and the Adult Dependants' Allowance so you may not receive the maximum amount of grant if you have a dependant whose income is above the threshold. If you are married, your spouse's income will be taken into account. If your spouse earns more than about £5,000 a year, you may not get any Childcare Grant.

How Do I Apply?

The financial assessment form the LEA will send you asks if you would like further information on help with childcare costs. If you tick 'YES', your LEA will send you further information and an application form for the Childcare Grant. You need to complete the application form and ask your childcare provider to complete the confirmation form with their contact and registration details, and confirmation of the amounts you pay.

How is it Paid?

The Childcare Grant is usually paid in three instalments along with your student loan by SLC. However, you will need to keep receipts for the amounts you have paid to your childcare provider as the LEA will require them, usually in February. This is so that they can verify you are being paid the right amount. If there is an underpayment, or your childcare costs have increased, they can amend their records and instruct SLC to either increase future payments or make an additional payment. In the event that your costs have been lower than originally estimated, they will reduce future payments of Childcare Grant. If this means that the reduction is more than the amount of Childcare Grant that would be payable, they may reduce future Parents' Learning Allowance payments. If this is the case, your LEA will advise you at the time.

SEE ALSO
Chapter 6 – particularly the sections on state benefits and tax credits
Chapter 12 – discretionary funding available from your university

Other Funding for Some Students from England

Social Work Bursaries

The Government has recently reformed social work education in England. As part of this, they introduced a new, non-means-tested bursary for students studying degree courses in Social Work. All 'home' students on social work degree courses are eligible for the bursary, which is paid for each year of the course.

How Do I Apply?

You first need to apply to your LEA for student support funding. When you have received the Financial Assessment form, you then apply to the General Social Care Council for the bursary. Application forms are available from your university and can also be downloaded from the General Social Care Council website at www.gscc.org.uk. Your university needs to complete part of the form to confirm that you have been accepted for a place on a social work degree course.

How Much Will I Get?

As the bursary is not means-tested, it is not affected by your, your parents' or your partner's income. There are three different rates of bursary, along the same lines as the student loan.

Social Work Bursary Rates (2003/04)	
Students living in London	£2,900
Students living outside London	£2,500
Students living with their parents	£2,100

In addition, there is a flat-rate placement travel grant of £500. The maximum bursary payable, including the travel grant, is therefore £3,400.

How Will I be Paid?

Payment arrangements had not been confirmed at the time of writing so check with your university or the General Social Care Council.

Opportunity Bursaries

WARNING!

2003 is the last year that new Opportunity Bursaries will be allocated. From September 2004, they are being replaced with a new Higher Education Grant that will be available from the LEA. The new grant is worth £1,000 per year if your family's annual income is £10,000 or less. If your family's income is above £10,000 but less than £20,000, you will still qualify for some of the grant but details have yet to be finalised. There will also be no age restriction on the new grant, unlike Opportunity Bursaries. For more information on the new HE Grant, contact your LEA after February 2004.

Opportunity Bursaries are grants, administered by universities on behalf of the Government, to encourage students from low-income families to go to university. The bursary is worth £2,000 over three years – if you are eligible, you receive £1,000 in the first year of study and £500 in each of the second and third years. If your course is only two years long, you receive a total of £1,500, paid as £1,000 in year one and £500 in year two. If your course is longer than three years, you will not receive any payments after the third year. To qualify for an Opportunity Bursary, you must meet all the following criteria:

- Be aged 20 or under on 1 September 2003
- Be the first person from your family to go to university (or, if you have a brother or sister already at university, no other member of your family must hold a degree-level award)
- Meet the residency criteria for student support as outlined in Chapter 1
- Your parents' combined gross income, including any state benefits or tax credits, must be less than £21,000
- You must attend a state school or college in an 'Excellence Challenge' area – your school or college should be able to tell you if this applies to you

In addition, if you have received an Education Maintenance Allowance between the ages of 16 and 19, this can be a good indication that you might qualify for an Opportunity Bursary. If you have attended a university summer school, or your school or college has a 'Compact' agreement with the university you will be going to, that may also mean you qualify for an Opportunity Bursary.

The Opportunity Bursary is only available to students from Excellence Challenge areas in England and is only available at universities in England. The HE Grant, for new students from September 2004, will be available to students from low-income families throughout England, wherever in the UK they choose to study.

How Do I Apply?

You apply to the university where you hold a 'firm' offer after applying through UCAS. You should apply as early as possible as each university only has a limited number of bursaries to offer – do not wait until you have received exam results and know which university you will be going to as all the funding may have been awarded by then. The bursary is transferable, meaning that if you originally apply to, for example, the University of Nottingham but actually go to the University of Brighton, you will still receive the bursary. You would not need to make a new application to the new university – just show them the letter from the university that made the award and they will make the necessary arrangements to pay the bursary to you.

How is it Paid?

Payment methods vary between universities. Some will pay a single lump sum and others pay the bursary in instalments – usually two. Some universities will pay by cheque and others by BACS – your university will tell you how the bursary is paid.

Other Funding for Some Students from Wales

Assembly Learning Grants

Assembly Learning Grants were introduced in September 2002 by the Welsh Assembly Government to provide additional support to students from low-income families. The grant is available to both new and existing students. It is paid in addition to the student loan and does not have to be repaid. It is available to students on both full-time and part-time courses, although part-time students must be studying at least 30 credit points in the academic year to qualify.

Assembly Learning Grant – How Much			
Parents' income ▶ Mode of study ▼	Below £5,000	£5,001–£10,000	£10,001–£15,000
Full-time	£1,500	£750	£450
Part-time	£750	£450	£300

The amount you get will depend on your parents' residual income, which is looked at in the same way as for the student loan and tuition fees.

How Do I Apply?

Remember, the Assembly Learning Grant is only available to students from Wales. You need to apply to your LEA. However, if you qualify for the ALG, you will receive it irrespective of which country of the UK you study in.

How is it Paid?

Assembly Learning Grants are usually paid by LEAs in three instalments. They are normally paid by cheque which you collect from your university.

You can get more information about the Assembly Learning Grant from your LEA or from the Welsh Assembly website at www.learning. wales.gov.uk. There is a version of this site in Welsh at www.dysgu. cymru.gov.uk

---

Parents Pay Attention! – How You Can Help

- Fill in the financial assessment form as soon as possible after it arrives
- Have details of your income to hand as this will make filling in the form much easier
- Encourage your son or daughter to make their applications as early as possible – they will be calling *you* if they do not have access to money when they enrol at university. . .

Quick Guide – Student Support Funding in England and Wales

- Apply as early as possible to your LEA
- Make sure you answer all the questions on the application forms and supply copies of all relevant documents – your loan may be delayed if you do not!
- Find out if you qualify for any of the additional grants or Opportunity Bursaries, HE Grants (England) or Assembly Learning Grants (Wales)
- Open a bank account before applying for your student loan – SLC need your bank details so they can pay you!
- Send your loan request to SLC as soon as you can to make sure you can access your student loan as soon as possible after you have enrolled on your course

3

Show Me the Money! (Part Two)

Statutory Funding for Students from Scotland

What Might You Get?

Funding for students from Scotland differs from that available to students from England and Wales. It also depends on where in the UK you will be studying.

Summary of What is Available

All Students

- Student loan of up to £4,000 (at 2003/04 rates), depending on where you study and on your, your parents' or partner's income (if you will be studying in London, the maximum student loan is £4,930)
- Additional help if you have dependants
- Additional help if you are disabled

If You Will Be Studying in Scotland

- No tuition fees to pay
- Some students will be eligible for a Young Students' Bursary and Additional Student Loan

If You Will Be Studying in Northern Ireland, Wales or England

- Help with tuition fees, depending on your parents', your partner's or your income
- Some students will be eligible for a Young Students' Outside Scotland Bursary

WARNING!

The information in this chapter only applies to students who started their courses in September 2001 or later. If you started your course before this date, please refer to the Student Awards Agency for Scotland's (SAAS) website at www.saas.gov.uk for information.

If You Will Be Studying in Scotland

The support you get will depend on whether you are classified as a 'young' student or a 'mature' student. If:

- you are aged under 25 and are not married on the first day of the first academic year of your course, or
- you have not been supporting yourself with earnings or benefits for any three years before starting the course, or
- you have no living parents and are aged under 25 at the start of the course, then you will be classified as a 'young' student.

In all other cases, you will be classified as a 'mature' student.

Young Students

The support package for young students is made up of a student loan, Young Students' Bursary and an additional loan. Much of this package is means-tested so you may not receive all of it if your, your parents' or your partner's income is above a certain level.

Student Loans

The student loan has two elements – a non-means-tested element and a means-tested element. This means that, even if your parents are very well off, you can qualify for the non-means-tested element of the loan provided you meet the eligibility criteria outlined in Chapter 1. The amount you get will also depend on whether you live in your parents' home or in halls, rented or your own accommodation. The maximum rates of student loan for Scottish students studying in Scotland in 2003/04 is as follows (final-year rates in brackets):

	Non Means Tested	Means Tested	Maximum Available
Halls of residence or rented accommodation	£790 (£680)	£3,210 (£2,790)	£4,000 (£3,470)
Living with parents	£520 (£420)	£2,645 (£2,345)	£3,165 (£2,765)

If you have to attend your course for more than 30 weeks and 3 days in an academic year, you may qualify for additional weeks' loan payments for each extra week you have to attend:

- £71 per week if you are not living in your parents' home
- £48 per week if you are living in your parents' home

> **EXAMPLE**
>
> **Heather's academic year is 34 weeks long.**
> **Assuming she gets the full student loan and is not living with her parents or in the final year of her course, her maximum entitlement is therefore:**
>
> | | | |
> |---|---|---|
> | Student loan | | £4,000 |
> | Additional weeks | 4 x £71 | £284 |
> | Total loan | | £4,284 |

Any contribution (see below) that your parents or partner are assessed as having to make will go directly to reducing your loan, since Scottish students studying in Scotland are entitled to free tuition.

Young Students' Bursary

The Young Students' Bursary replaces part of the student loan for those students who are eligible. This means that if you qualify for the bursary you will have to pay back less after you complete your course. The bursary is fully means-tested so the amount you will get depends on your family's income. To be eligible for the bursary, you must fulfil *all* of the following criteria:

- You must be eligible for help with your tuition fees
- You must have started your course in the 2001/02 academic year, or later
- You must be resident in Scotland and studying in Scotland
- You must have been aged under 25 on the first day of the first academic year of your course

- You must not have been married on the first day of the first academic year of your course
- You must not have been supporting yourself through earnings or state benefits for any three years before starting your course
- Your course must be a full-time higher-education course (e.g. degree, HND)

The amount of bursary you can get is not affected by where you live whilst studying – there is one rate regardless of whether you live with your parents or in halls or rented accommodation. However, the bursary is dependent on your family's income. If your family's income is above £27,200 per year, you will not qualify for the Young Students' Bursary. If your family's income is below £10,490 per year, you will get the maximum bursary of £2,100. If your family's income is between £10,490 and £27,200 per year, you will qualify for a proportion of the bursary, provided you meet all the other eligibility criteria.

EXAMPLE

Thomas lives with his parents who are both retired and receiving state benefits. Their income is below £10,490 per year.
Thomas would qualify for the 'Parental Home' rate of loan of £3,165.
He qualifies for a Young Students' Bursary of £2,100.
His support package is therefore:

Student loan	£1,065
Bursary	£2,100
Total	£3,165

EXAMPLE

Shona lives with her mother who earns £18,000 per year. Shona lives in halls of residence whilst studying.
Her maximum loan entitlement is £4,000
She is entitled to a bursary of £998
Shona's support package is therefore:

Student loan	£3,002
Bursary	£998
Total	£4,000

EXAMPLE

Hugh's parents earn £26,000 per year. Hugh lives in private rented accommodation whilst studying.

His maximum loan entitlement is	£4,000
His parents are expected to contribute	£603
Making his maximum loan	£3,397

As Hugh's parents earn less than £27,200 per year, he is entitled to a Young Students' Bursary of £131
Hugh's support package is therefore:

Parental contribution	£603
Student loan	£3,266
Bursary	£131
Total	£4,000

Additional Loan

If you are eligible for a Young Students' Bursary, you may also qualify for an additional loan. If your family's income is below £15,730, the maximum additional loan is £520. The amount of the additional loan is reduced as family income increases until an income level of £18,800 when it becomes zero.

In the cases of the above three examples:

– Thomas would be entitled to an additional loan of £520 as his family's income is below £15,730.
– Shona would be entitled to an additional loan of £142 as her family's income is below £18,800.
– Hugh would not be entitled to the additional loan as his family's income is above the £18,800 threshold.

Mature Students

Mature students can apply for the student loan in the same way as young students. Mature students are not, however, entitled to Young Students' Bursaries or additional loans. Instead, if you meet the relevant criteria, you can apply to your university or college for assistance from the Mature Students' Bursary Fund. The scheme is operated differently amongst universities and colleges so you will need to check with your place of study whether you would receive assistance. Generally speaking, you will be eligible to apply for assistance from the Mature Students' Bursary Fund if:

- You are a UK resident
- You are studying at a publicly funded Scottish university or college
- You started your course in the 2001/02 academic year, or later
- You have taken out your full student loan entitlement
- You were aged 25 or over on the first day of the first academic year of your course, or you were married by the first day of your course, or you had been supporting yourself through earnings or state benefits for at least three years before starting your course

If you have already done a course of higher education and received support from public funds, whether it was a grant or a loan, you will not be eligible for a payment from the Mature Students' Bursary Fund. Payments from the fund can be made for the following costs:

- Registered or formal childcare – this follows the same rules as the Childcare Grant in England, Wales and Northern Ireland
- Housing costs
- Excess travel costs that cannot be reclaimed from SAAS – for example the costs involved in taking children to and from the place of childcare
- A 'Mature Student Premium' of up to £150 for other unspecified costs

In 2002/03, the maximum amount available from the Mature Students' Bursary Fund was £2,000 but this is under review for 2003/04. If you would like to find out more about the fund, contact the student services department of your university or college in Scotland.

The Graduate Endowment

Tuition for Scottish and European Union students who study in Scotland is free of charge. However, some students may have to pay the Graduate Endowment once they have completed their course. The Graduate Endowment is a contribution that recognises the higher education benefits you have received, and the money paid goes towards the student support scheme in Scotland. There are certain groups who do not have to pay the Graduate Endowment and these are currently:

- Those assessed as independent of their parents at the start of the course
- Students who have received a Lone Parents' Grant or Disabled Students' Allowance at some point during the course
- Students on HNC or HND courses or those who transferred from HNC/D to degree courses before 2001/02
- Students who complete a degree in less than two years having already completed a HNC/D, or who complete the degree in less than three years in all other cases
- Students who received a means-tested Scottish Executive Health Department bursary
- Those who do not receive a degree award or are studying outside Scotland
- Those who study part-time

The amount payable is currently £2,300, although this does increase in line with inflation each year. If you do have to pay the Graduate Endowment, SAAS will write to you during your final year to tell you how you can pay it, and again shortly before you complete the course to find out exactly how you plan to pay it. There are currently three ways of paying the Graduate Endowment:

- In a lump sum to SAAS
- By taking out an additional student loan for the full amount
- By paying part to SAAS and taking out an additional student loan for the remainder

This additional loan operates under the same terms and conditions, for repayment purposes, as the student loan for living costs.

If You Will Be Studying Elsewhere in the UK

Grants for Tuition Fees

The maximum fee that can be charged for 'home' students on a full-time course in 2003/04 is £1,125. However, you may find you are entitled to some help from SAAS towards paying the tuition fees. When you complete your application form to SAAS (form SAS3 or via the SAAS website at www.saas.gov.uk), make sure you include details of your family income. SAAS need this information so they can undertake an income assessment, more commonly known as a means test. If the information is not provided, you will have to pay the full tuition fee and you will receive only the non-means-tested student loan.

There are complex rules on how family contributions work, the main points of which are outlined in the table below.

Contributions – How They Work (2003/04 rates shown)

If you are assessed as dependent on your parents	For residual income below £20,970, NO CONTRIBUTION. For a residual income of £20,970, a contribution of £45 which then increases until approx. £30,690 when a full contribution to tuition fees will be assessed.
If you have a partner	For residual income below £17,830, NO CONTRIBUTION. For a residual income of £17,830, a contribution of £45 which then increases until approx. £27,690 when a full contribution to tuition fees will be assessed.
If you are an independent student	The first £7,500 of certain income is ignored, and there are some allowances for income such as sponsorship, part-time work during your course and certain benefits. If income is above this level, you are expected to make a contribution, pound for pound.

You are probably wondering what residual income actually means. Contrary to popular belief, it is not income minus tax and National Insurance payments. Broadly speaking, it refers to gross income with deductions made for pension payments that qualify for tax relief, other adult dependants, a parent who is also a student and certain other deductions that will only apply to a very small number of people – SAAS can give you more information. In the case of parents or partners, SAAS will look at income from the previous tax year, 2003/04 for students starting courses in September 2004. If the income is likely to be significantly lower in the year you will be studying, you can ask SAAS to look again at your application, taking into account the new information. If you are classed as an independent student, you will need to estimate your income for the year you will be studying.

You become liable to pay the maximum fee of £1,125 in the following cases:

● Your parents' residual income is approximately £30,690 or higher; or
● Your partner's residual income is £27,690 or higher; or
● If you are classed as an independent student, your income during the year you will be studying is greater than £7,500 by £1,125 or more; or
● You decide not to apply for means-tested support

(Remember, these are 2003/04 rates so if you are starting your course after September 2003, they will probably be increased in line with inflation.)

Many students do not realise that, once their eligibility has been confirmed, they need to provide further income details in order to have their fee liability assessed. There are, as ever, some exceptions to these rules – especially if you have a brother or sister who is also at university, or if there are other children for whom your parents are responsible. If this applies to you, ask SAAS for more information.

Remember, if your parents do not give details of their income (and under the Family Law (Scotland) Act 1985, they have a general obligation to support their children aged between 18 and 25 who are in further education or training) and you will be studying outside Scotland, you will not have your fees paid and you will only be entitled to the reduced rate non-means-tested student loan.

So How Do I Get Help with Paying My Fees?

Apply to SAAS – the same form is used to apply for a grant for fees, a student loan and any additional grants (except Disabled Students' Allowances).

How are My Fees Paid?

If you have to pay all or some of the tuition fees yourself, your university will tell you how and when to pay.

If SAAS are paying some or all of the tuition fees on your behalf, they will instruct the Student Loans Company (SLC) to pay the fees direct to your university.

SEE ALSO
Chapter 10 – Tuition fees and other course costs
Chapter 13 – Dealing with Debt

Student Loans

The student loan has two elements – a non-means-tested element and a means-tested element. This means that, even if your parents are very well off, you can qualify for the non-means-tested element of the loan, provided you meet the eligibility criteria outlined in Chapter 1. Maximum student loan rates for students from Scotland who are studying elsewhere in the UK in 2003/04 are (final-year figures are in brackets):

	Non Means Tested	Means Tested	Maximum Available
London	£2,065 (£1,940)	£2,865 (£2,335)	£4,930 (£4,275)
Outside London	£1,915 (£1,805)	£2,085 (£1,665)	£4,000 (£3,470)
Living with parents	£1,645 (£1,545)	£1,520 (£1,220)	£3,165 (£2,765)

If you study at a campus of a university in London and do not live with your parents whilst studying, you will qualify for the London rate of loan. If you study outside London and do not live with your parents you will qualify for the Outside London rate of loan (usually referred to as the 'Elsewhere' rate). If you live with your parents, you will qualify for the 'Parental Home' rate of loan, regardless of where you study.

If you receive the means-tested loan and have to attend your course for more than 30 weeks, not including vacations, you may receive an extra amount of loan as follows:

- £92 per week if you get the London rate of loan
- £71 per week if you get the Elsewhere rate of loan
- £48 per week if you get the Parental Home rate of loan

You do not need to make a separate application for the extra weeks' loan as it should be added automatically to your loan entitlement by SAAS from the information they have about courses at your particular university.

EXAMPLE

Martina gets the London rate of loan and she has to attend her course for 35 weeks of the year. If she gets the full means-tested loan, she is therefore entitled to:

London rate loan	£4,930
Extra weeks (5)	£460
Full loan entitlement	£5,390

The means test used for student loans is the same as for tuition fees. You already know that if, for example, your parents' income is higher than about £30,690 then they are assessed as liable to pay the full tuition fee. But what if their income is above this level? The answer is that the means-tested loan, including any extra weeks' loan, starts to be reduced. If you are assessed on the basis of your partner's income, this threshold is £27,690.

EXAMPLE

Michael is going to a university outside London and will be living in halls of residence. His course has three extra weeks. His parents have a residual income of £38,000. Before the means test, Michael's maximum loan entitlement would be as follows:

Non-means-tested loan (Elsewhere rate)	£1,915
Means-tested loan (Elsewhere rate)	£2,085
Extra weeks' loan (3 weeks @ £71 each)	£213
Total	£4,213

Since Andrew's parents have an income of £38,000, and the threshold is £30,690, his means-tested loan is reduced by £812. His total loan entitlement is therefore £3,401.

EXAMPLE

Donald will be going to a university outside London and living in halls of residence. If he were entitled to the maximum means-tested loan, he would get £4,000. However, his parents' residual income is £62,000.

This means that their assessed contribution is £5,371. The first £1,125 of this contribution is towards tuition fees. His loan will be reduced by £2,085 so that he receives the non-means-tested element of £1,915. This is the absolute minimum he can get, even though the assessed parental contribution is greater.

How Do I Apply for the Loan?

You apply using form SAS3 from SAAS. You can also apply online via the SAAS website (see Appendix A). They will notify the Student Loans Company of your application and you will then receive a letter from SLC giving the details of your loan and how and when it will be paid.

When Should I Apply?

Do not wait until you have final exam results and know which university you are going to. The application process can take several weeks or months, so if your course starts in the autumn, your filled-in forms should be with SAAS by the middle of the May before you start your course.

How is the Loan Paid?

The loan is usually paid in three instalments if you apply to SAAS in the first term of the academic year; in two instalments if you apply in the second term and in one lump sum if you apply in the third term. Second and third instalments are always paid by BACS transfer directly into your bank account. In September 2003, some students will receive their first instalment by BACS and others by cheque as some universities are taking part in a pilot scheme to pay first instalments by BACS. It is expected that all students will receive first instalments by BACS in September 2004.

Young Students Outside Scotland Bursaries

If you are assessed as a young student and your parents' income is below £18,800 per year, you may qualify for a Young Students' Outside Scotland Bursary of up to £520 (2003/04 rates). To be eligible for the bursary you must fulfil *all* the following conditions:

- You must be eligible for help with your tuition fees
- You must have started your course in the 2002/03 academic year, or later
- You must be resident in Scotland and studying outside Scotland
- You must have been aged under 25 on the first day of the first academic year of your course
- You must not have been married on the first day of the first academic year of your course
- You must not have been supporting yourself through earnings or state benefits for any three years before starting your course
- Your course must be a full-time higher-education course (e.g. degree, HND)

The amount of bursary you can get is not affected by where you live whilst studying – there is one rate regardless of whether you live with your parents or in halls or rented accommodation. However, the bursary is dependent on your family's income. If your family's income is above £18,800 per year, you will not qualify for the bursary. If your family's income is below £15,000 per year, you will get the maximum bursary of £520. If your family's income is between £15,000 and £18,800 per year, you will qualify for a proportion of the bursary, provided you meet all the other eligibility criteria.

EXAMPLE

Lisa has lived in Scotland all her life and will be going to a university in Wales. Her parents earn £13,000 per year.

Lisa qualifies for the full means-tested student loan of £4,000 and full assistance with tuition fees.

She will also receive a Young Students' Outside Scotland Bursary of £520.

EXAMPLE

Douglas has lived in Scotland all his life and will be going to university in London. His parents earn £16,000 per year.

Douglas qualifies for the full means-tested student loan of £4,930 and full assistance with tuition fees.

He will also receive a Young Students' Outside Scotland Bursary of £475.

EXAMPLE

Monica has lived in Scotland all her life and will be going to university in Northern Ireland. Her parents earn £20,000 per year.

Monica will receive the full means-tested student loan of £4,000 and will get full assistance with tuition fees. However, she will not receive a Young Students' Outside Scotland Bursary as her parents' income is above the threshold.

Quick Guide – Tuition Fees and Student Loans

- Apply to SAAS from January 2003 (January 2004 if you are starting your course in September 2004)
- Make sure you fill in the form with all the necessary details and return it to SAAS by the middle of May before you start your course (assuming you start in the autumn term)
- Open a bank account before going to university so it is ready to receive your first student loan payment

SEE ALSO
Chapter 8 – bank accounts
Chapter 15 – repaying your loan

Other Funding

The following types of funding are not affected by where in the UK you are studying.

Disabled Students' Allowances

Disabled Students' Allowances for students from Scotland operate in much the same way as those available to students from England and Wales. Applications are handled by SAAS using form DSA F/T. For more information on DSA, refer to Chapter 2.

Care Leavers' Grant

The Care Leavers' Grant is a non-repayable grant that can be paid to some students who were in care for at least three months following their 16th birthday and are aged under 21 on starting their courses. It is intended to cover the costs of accommodation during the long summer vacation and is worth up to £100 per week, depending on the actual cost of the accommodation.

How Do I Apply?

To SAAS.

How is it Paid?

Care Leavers' Grant is paid for the long summer vacation only. SAAS will give you more information on how they will pay the grant if you are eligible.

Grants for Dependants

If you have another adult or child who is financially dependent on you, you may qualify for a Dependants' Grant. It is means-tested and the amount you actually receive will depend on your income and the income of your dependants. There are different rates for dependants of different ages. For 2003/04, the maximum grant rates are as shown on page 57.

If your dependants have any income of their own, it will be taken into account and may reduce any grant you receive. Any award of the Dependants' Grant is made on a provisional basis. At the end of the year you will need to confirm to SAAS the income your dependants have received, and they will calculate a final entitlement to the Dependants' Grant. If you have received more grant than your final entitlement, you will have to repay the difference.

Dependant	Maximum Rate (2003/04)
Husband or wife who is financially dependent upon you, or other adult for whom you have legal responsibility who is on a low income	£2,280
First child if you do not have an adult dependant	£2,280
Children aged 18 or over on the first day of the academic year	£1,825
Children aged over 16 but under 18 on the first day of the academic year	£1,270
Children aged over 11 but under 16 on the first day of the academic year	£950
Children aged 11 or under on the first day of the course	£475

School Meals Grant

If you receive a Dependants' Grant for children under 16, and neither you nor your partner still receive Income Support or Income-based Jobseekers' Allowance whilst you are studying, you may also receive a School Meals Grant:

- £260 for each child aged 3–10 on the first day of the academic year
- £280 for each child aged 11–16 on the first day of the academic year

Lone Parents' Grant

If you are a lone parent and receive a Dependants' Grant, you may also receive a Lone Parents' Grant of £1,125.

Additional Childcare Grant for Lone Parents

If you receive the Lone Parents' Grant and have to pay for registered or formal childcare whilst you are studying, you can receive an additional grant of up to £1,050 per year, depending on the cost of the childcare.

EXAMPLE

Sally has three children, aged 6, 12 and 17. She is a lone parent. She will be entitled to the following grants (in addition to the student loan and assistance with tuition fees):

Dependants' Grant for first child	£2,280
Dependants' Grant for 12-year-old	£950
Dependants' Grant for 7-year-old	£475
School Meals Grant for 12-year-old	£280
School Meals Grant for 7-year-old	£260
Lone Parents' Grant	£1,125
Total	£5,370

(If Sally uses registered childcare she may also qualify for the Additional Childcare Grant, and if she studies in Scotland she may qualify for additional support from the Mature Students' Bursary Fund.)

How Do I Apply?

Your application to SAAS includes questions about dependants so make sure you fill in the relevant sections. If you are entitled to the Additional Childcare Grant, SAAS will send you another form to allow you to give details of your childcare costs and childcare provider.

How Will I Be Paid?

All the grants mentioned above are paid in three instalments at the same time as your student loan.

Travelling Expenses

You can claim travelling expenses whilst you are attending your course. This assistance is fully means-tested so the amount you actually receive will depend on your own or your family's income. SAAS will not pay the first £155 of your travel expenses and will expect you to use the cheapest possible method of transport, using student concessions and discounts wherever possible. You will need to keep all your receipts as SAAS may ask for evidence that you have actually bought travel tickets. Air fares will only be paid if your home is in one of the offshore islands, and they will not pay for taxi fares, car parking, sleeper berths or food for the journey. The maximum amounts that will be paid are as follows:

Single students living at home	£790 per year (i.e. £945–£155)
Independent students living in their own home	£930 per year
Students living away from home	£3 per day plus the cost of one return journey to parents' home per term, less the first £155
Students living away from home in London	£3.50 per day plus the cost of one return journey to parents' home per term, less the first £155

EXAMPLE

Rani will be studying in London. Her return journey to London from her home in Falkirk costs £65. It costs her £1.40 per day to get to and from university.

Journeys home	£195
Travel to university (30 weeks)	£210
Subtotal	£405
LESS the first	£155
Travel expenses payable	£250

How Do I Apply?

SAAS encourage students to make applications for travel expenses via their website (www.saas.gov.uk) although application forms are also sent to universities and colleges for students who prefer to fill in a paper form. You should send this form to SAAS as soon as possible after the end of the first term.

How Will I Be Paid?

SAAS will pay travel expenses directly into your bank account so you must give them your bank details when you fill in the application form.

Parents Pay Attention! – How You Can Help

- Fill in the SAS3 or online form as soon as possible
- Have details of your income to hand as this will make filling in the form much easier
- Encourage your son or daughter to make their applications as early as possible – they will be calling *you* if they do not have access to money when they enrol at university

4 Show Me the Money! (Part Three)

Statutory Funding for Students from Northern Ireland

What Might You Get?

Summary of What is Available

- Student loan of up to £4,930 (at 2003/04 rates), depending on where you study and on your, your parents' or partner's income
- Assistance with tuition fees of up to £1,125 (at 2003/04 rates), depending on your, your parents' or your partner's income
- Additional help if you have a disability, known as a Disabled Students' Allowance
- Additional help if you have an adult dependant
- Additional help if you have dependant children
- Students from low-income families may qualify for a Higher Education Bursary of up to £2,000 which replaces part of the student loan

Not all students will qualify for all of the above funding as some grants are only available to certain groups of students. However, all students can apply for grants for tuition fees and student loans.

Grants for Tuition Fees

Grants for tuition fees work in the same way as for students from England and Wales – refer to Chapter 2.

From the information on your form and the documents sent with it, which can include P60s and/or payslips, your Education and Library Board (ELB) will work out whether or not you (or your parents or partner) have to make a contribution towards tuition fees. There are complex rules on how the contributions work which differ from those for students from England and Wales as shown in the table below.

Contributions for Students from Northern Ireland How They Work (2003/04 rates shown)	
If you are assessed as dependent on your parents	For residual income below £20,970, NO CONTRIBUTION. For a residual income of £20,970, a contribution of £45. Contribution increases by £1 for each £12.50 of additional residual income.
If you have a partner	For residual income below £20,970, NO CONTRIBUTION. For a residual income of £20,970, a contribution of £45. Contribution increases by £1 for each £8 of additional residual income.
If you are an independent student	The first £7,500 of certain income is ignored, and there are some allowances for income such as sponsorship, part-time work during your course and certain benefits. If income is above this level, you are expected to make a contribution, pound for pound.

You become liable to pay the maximum fee of £1,125 in the following cases:

● Your parents' residual income is £34,470; or
● Your partner's residual income is £29,610; or
● If you are classed as an independent student, your income during

the year you will be studying is greater than £7,500 by more than £1,125 or more; or

● You decide not to apply for means-tested support.

Remember that these are 2003/04 rates. If you are starting your course after September 2004 the rates will be increased in line with inflation.

Remember, you must apply to your ELB and fill in an income-assessment form for them to be able to decide whether or not you have to pay any tuition fees.

Partners or parents who are assessed as liable to make a contribution are expected by the Government to actually make it. However, there is no legal compulsion on them to pay up, which leaves some students with reduced amounts of loans and bills from their universities for tuition fees. If this happens to you, speak to a student adviser or welfare officer at your university or students' union.

How do I Apply?

Apply to your ELB – the same form is used for applying for a grant for fees, a student loan and any additional grants (except Disabled Students' Allowances).

How is it Paid?

If you have to pay all or some of the tuition fees yourself, your university will tell you how and when to pay.

If your ELB are paying some or all of the tuition fees on your behalf, they will instruct the Student Loans Company (SLC) to pay the fees direct to your university.

SEE ALSO
Chapter 10 – paying for your studies
Chapter 13 – dealing with debt

Student Loans

The student loan has two elements – a non-means-tested element and a means-tested element. This means that, even if your parents are very well off, you can qualify for the non-means-tested element of the loan, provided you meet the eligibility criteria outlined in Chapter 1. A higher proportion of the student loan for students from Northern Ireland is means-tested than for students from England and Wales. There are three different rates of loan, depending on whether you will be living with your parents whilst studying, in rented accommodation in the London area or elsewhere. Maximum student loan rates for students from Northern Ireland in 2003/04 are (final-year figures are in brackets):

	Non Means Tested	Means Tested	Maximum Available
London	£3,604 (£2,949)	£1,326 (£1,326)	£4,930 (£4,275)
Outside London	£2,674 (£2,144)	£1,326 (£1,326)	£4,000 (£3,470)
Living with parents	£1,839 (£1,439)	£1,326 (£1,326)	£3,165 (£2,765)

If you receive the means-tested loan and have to attend your course for more than 30 weeks, not including vacations, you may receive an extra amount of loan as follows:

- £92 per week if you get the London rate of loan
- £71 per week if you get the Elsewhere rate of loan
- £48 per week if you get the Parental Home rate of loan

You do not need to make a separate application for the extra weeks' loan as it should be added automatically to your loan entitlement by your ELB from the information they have about courses at your particular university.

How Do I Apply?

1. You first apply to your ELB for an eligibility assessment.
2. Once the ELB has decided that you are eligible for support, they will send you a financial assessment form which you complete and return. They will then work out whether any contribution to either fees or the student loan is due.
3. The ELB then write to you to tell you how much of the tuition fees they will pay and how much student loan you can apply for. You will be sent three copies – one for you to keep and one to give to the university. Fill in the back of the third copy as this is the Loan Request Form, and send it to SLC at least one month before you are due to start your course, if possible.

This applies to 'new' students making their first application for student support. Students in the second and subsequent years do not need to complete another eligibility form but they do need to fill in a financial assessment form in order to qualify for means-tested support.

When Should I Apply?

Do not wait until you have final exam results and know which university you are going to. The application process can take several weeks or months. For example, if you are starting your course in September, your eligibility assessment form should be sent to your ELB by the middle of the preceding March at the latest, and the financial-assessment form by mid-June at the latest. You will need to send your Loan Request form to SLC at least one month before the start of your course to guarantee payment of the loan at the start of the autumn term.

How is it Paid?

The loan is usually paid in three instalments if you apply to the SLC in the first term of the academic year; in two instalments if you apply in the second term and in one lump sum if you apply in the third term. Second and third instalments are always paid by BACS transfer directly into your bank account. In September 2003, some students will receive their first instalment by BACS and others by cheque as some universities are taking part in a pilot scheme to pay first instalments by BACS. It is expected that all students will receive first instalments by BACS in September 2004.

Quick Guide – Tuition Fees and Student Loans

- Apply to your ELB from January 2003 (January 2004 if you are starting your course in September 2004)
- Complete both the eligibility and income-assessment forms to see if you have to pay any tuition fees or make a contribution to your living costs
- Apply to SLC for the loan as early as you can
- Open a bank account before going to university so it is ready to receive your first student loan payment

SEE ALSO
Chapter 8 – bank accounts
Chapter 15 – repaying your loan

Additional Grants

If you are disabled, you may be eligible for a Disabled Students' Allowance. If you have dependants, you may qualify for additional grants. These work in the same way as grants for students from England and Wales, so for more information refer to Chapter 2.

Higher Education Bursaries

Students from families with low incomes, below £20,000 per year, may qualify for a Higher Education Bursary which does not have to be repaid. You must be eligible for student support, as outlined in Chapter 1, and studying on a full-time course. The amount of bursary you receive depends on your own or your family's income, so if you think you might qualify it is important that you and your parents complete the income assessment form from the ELB. The maximum amount of bursary available is £2,000, and if you receive this your entitlement to a student loan is reduced by £1,500. You will qualify for the maximum amount of bursary if your family income is below £10,000. If you qualify for a lower amount of bursary, your student loan entitlement is reduced by the same amount. This means that students who receive the highest amount of bursary will receive an additional £500 of support which does not have to be repaid.

How Do I Apply?

Your ELB will assess your entitlement to the bursary at the same time as they assess entitlement to assistance with tuition fees and for a student loan.

How is it Paid?

The bursary is usually paid in three instalments, one at the start of each term. Your ELB will make the payments either by BACS directly into your bank account or by cheque which you collect from your university.

Parents Pay Attention! – How You Can Help

- Fill in the financial assessment form as soon as possible
- Have details of your income to hand as this will make filling in the form much easier
- Encourage your son or daughter to make their applications as early as possible – they will be calling *you* if they do not have access to money when they enrol at university

Quick Guide – Student-supported Funding in Northern Ireland

- Apply as early as possible to your ELB
- Make sure you answer all the questions on the application forms and supply copies of all relevant documents – your loan may be delayed if you do not!
- Find out if you qualify for any of the additional grants, or a Higher Education Bursary
- Open a bank account before applying for your student loan – SLC need your bank details so they can pay you!
- Send your loan request to SLC as soon as you can to make sure you can access your student loan as soon as possible after you have enrolled on your course

Money! That's What I Want!

Funding for Healthcare Students

Students on healthcare courses are funded differently to students on other courses of higher education in the United Kingdom. Healthcare courses include the following areas of study:

- Nursing and midwifery
- Operating-department practice
- Chiropody, dietetics, occupational therapy, physiotherapy, radiography, speech and language therapy, audiology
- Dental hygiene or dental therapy
- Medicine or dentistry if you are in Year 5 or later of the course or if you are in Year 2 or later of the accelerated graduate-entry medical or dentistry course (for earlier parts of the course, you apply to your LEA, ELB or SAAS as outlined in Chapters 2, 3 and 4)

To qualify for support, you must be accepted for an NHS-funded place by your university. If your course is not NHS-funded, you can apply to your LEA, ELB or SAAS for a student loan and assistance with tuition fees.

Where to Apply

This depends on the area of the UK in which you will be studying. You will note that this is different to the main student support system, where you apply to the authority where you live.

Students Who Will Study in England

Students from the UK who will study in England should apply to the NHS Student Grants Unit in Blackpool. Their contact details can be found in Appendix A. The funding you get will depend on whether your course is a diploma or degree-level qualification. Students from other EU countries can apply for a fees-only award that will cover their tuition fees but not provide any assistance with living costs. Students from overseas, who do not meet the residency requirements as outlined in Chapter 1, are not eligible for any assistance.

Degree-level Courses

These include most of the 'allied health professions' – briefly, anything other than medicine or dentistry, nursing, midwifery or operating-department practice, and nursing or midwifery degree-level courses. Students on these courses may qualify for:

- Means-tested bursaries
- Additional allowances if you have dependants or disabilities
- Reduced-rate student loans

Means-tested Bursaries The means-tested bursary provides an allowance towards day-to-day living costs, although it does not cover the full amount. As with the student loan, there are three rates – London, Elsewhere and Parental Home – depending on whether your university is in London or not and whether or not you live with your parents whilst on the course.

Bursary Rate	Amount per year (2003/04 rates)
London rate	£2,703
Elsewhere rate	£2,200
Parental Home rate	£1,800

In some cases, you might be entitled to additional payments, depending on your circumstances. As the bursary and additional allowances are fully means-tested, you may not receive the full amount shown in the following tables.

Extra Weeks' Allowance If your course requires attendance for more than 30 weeks and 3 days a year, you may qualify for Extra Weeks' Allowances for each additional week that you attend.

This is likely to apply to most people who qualify for the means-tested bursary as healthcare courses usually require a longer period of attendance each year than other courses. If you have to attend your course for more than 45 weeks in the year, your allowance will cover 52 weeks. Extra weeks' allowances are as follows:

- £92 per week if you receive the London rate of bursary
- £71 per week if you receive the Elsewhere rate of bursary
- £48 per week if you receive the Parental Home rate of bursary

Older Students' Allowance If you are aged at least 26 before the first academic year of your course, you may qualify for an Older Students' Allowance. The first day of the academic year is 1 September if you start your course between 1 September and 31 December; 1 January for courses starting between 1 January and 31 March; and 1 April in all other cases.

> **E X A M P L E**
>
> Florence is 26 on 3 August and will be starting an occupational therapy course on 8 September. As she is over 26 on 1 September that year, she qualifies for the Older Students' Allowance.
>
> Peter will be 26 on 8 October. He started his course on 28 September. Because he had not reached the age of 26 on 1 September, he does not qualify for the Older Students' Allowance.

If you receive the Older Students' Allowance at the start of the course, you will receive it for each subsequent year of the course at the same rate. For example, if you are aged 26 at the start of the course, you receive the Age 26 rate throughout – it does not increase each year in line with your age. Older Students' Allowance will not be paid if you receive the Single Parents' Addition.

Your age immediately before the start of the course	Amount per year (2003/04 rates)
26	£388
27	£671
28	£996
29+	£1,316

Dependants' Allowances If you have a partner, children or other adult family members who are financially dependent on you, you may qualify for a Dependants' Allowance. Their income will be taken into account when working out how much, if any, Dependants' Allowance you can receive. The amount you can get also depends on the age of the dependant in question.

Age of Dependant	Amount per year (2003/04 rates)
Spouse or other adult dependant, or first child if you do not have an adult dependant	£2,280
Child under 11 (Primary school age)	£477
Child aged 11–15	£954
Child aged 16–17	£1,269
Child aged 18 +	£1,825

Single Parent Addition Single students with dependant children may qualify for this additional allowance of £1,126. It cannot be paid to students who receive an Older Students' Allowance but the amount of the Single Parent Addition is higher than the Older Students' Allowance for students aged 28 or under at the start of the course. If you are aged 29 or more at the start of the course, the Older Students' Allowance is worth more to you, so you should claim that instead.

Two Homes Grant If you have a dependant and need to maintain a home, other than your term-time accommodation, you might qualify for this additional grant of £794.

Practice Placement Costs If you incur additional travel costs whilst undertaking clinical placements, you may qualify for assistance. The travel costs must be higher than you would normally pay to get to your place of study and you must normally use the cheapest method of transport, using any discounts or concessions available. If you need to use a car to get to your placement, you will need to get authority from your university before going on placement.

Disabled Students' Allowance Disabled Students' Allowances (DSAs) operate in the same way as for the main student-support system, except that they are administered by the NHS Student Grants Unit rather than LEAs. Information on the rates and what the allowances can cover can be found in Chapter 2. DSAs are not means-tested so the NHS will not look at you or your family's income, but they will require medical evidence.

How Do I Apply?

Once you have been accepted on an NHS-funded course, you need to make an application to the NHS Student Grants Unit (details in Appendix A). They will assess your entitlement and, once the university has notified them that you have started your course, they will write to tell you how much you are entitled to. You should receive this within 10 days of starting the course. The means test is broadly the same as for student support in England, as outlined in Chapter 2. The main exception is that any contribution will go towards the bursary as NHS-funded students do not have to pay tuition fees.

How Will I Be Paid?

The bursary and any additional grants will be paid monthly. The first instalment will cover the first two months and will be paid by cheque which you collect from your university. The remaining instalments will be paid by BACS transfer on a monthly basis, directly into your bank account.

Other Funding for Degree-level Students in England

Student Loans Healthcare students on degree courses can apply to their LEA for a reduced-rate student loan. As with the main student loan scheme, there are three different rates depending on where you will be living although these student loans are not means-tested. The LEA will not look at your own, your partner's or your parents' income. Final year students also receive a lower rate of loan.

Student Loan Rates for Means-tested NHS Bursary Holders (Final year rates are in brackets)	
London rate	£2,420 (£1,765)
Elsewhere rate	£1,960 (£1,430)
Parental Home rate	£1,500 (£1,100)

Repayment of student loans operates in the same way as for student loans paid under the main student support arrangements. Further details are in Chapter 15.

How Do I Apply?

You apply to your LEA who will tell you how much student loan you can take out. You then send the Loan Request Form to the Student Loans Company.

How Will I Be Paid?

Student loans are paid termly. The first instalment will usually be by BACS or, in some universities, by cheque. Instalments at the start of the second and third terms will be paid into your bank account by BACS.

Hardship Loans (2003/04 only) If you have taken the full means-tested bursary and student loan and are still in hardship, you may be able to apply to your university for a Hardship Loan of up to £500. More information can be found in Chapter 2.

Hardship Funds (2003/04) or Access to Learning Fund (2004 onwards) If you are still in hardship after taking a Hardship Loan, you may be able to apply to your university for assistance from the Hardship or Access to Learning Fund. More information on these funds can be found in Chapter 12.

NHS Hardship Grants If you have exhausted all other sources of funding and are in exceptional hardship, you may be eligible to apply to your university for an NHS Hardship Grant. You must be in receipt of a means-tested bursary and have taken the full student loan. Students from other EU countries who receive assistance only with tuition fees cannot apply for an NHS Hardship Grant.

SEE ALSO
Chapter 6 – sections on benefits and tax credits, and charitable trusts

Diploma-level Courses

UK students on diploma-level courses are eligible for a non-means-tested bursary. These are paid at much higher rates than means-tested bursaries as they are designed to cover your full living costs. As with degree-level courses, other EU students can apply for assistance with tuition fees, and overseas students are not eligible for any assistance.

The amount of bursary you receive is not dependent on your or your family's income so if you are eligible, you will get the full amount. Unlike the means-tested bursary, the non-means-tested bursary assumes that you need to attend your course for at least 45 weeks of the year so there are no extra weeks' allowances, unless you have to move to London to attend a practice placement. In this case, the bursary is increased by £17.00 a week for each week you attend the placement.

Bursary Rate	Amount per year (2003/04 rates)
London rate	£6,535
Elsewhere rate	£5,562
Parental Home rate	£5,562

Depending on your circumstances, you may also qualify for additional allowances:

Older Students' Allowance This has the same rules as the Older Students' Allowance in the means-tested bursary scheme, except there is only one rate, £650 at 2003/04 rates. You cannot receive this as well as the Single Parent Addition.

Dependants' Allowances If you have a partner, children or other adult family members who are financially dependent on you, you may qualify for a Dependants' Allowance. Their income will be taken into account when working out how much, if any, Dependants' Allowance you can receive. The amount you can get also depends on the age of the dependant in question.

Age of Dependant	Amount per year (2003/04 rates)
Spouse or other adult dependant, or first child if you do not have an adult dependant	£1,934
Child under 11 (Primary school age)	£409
Child aged 11–15	£813
Child aged 16–17	£1,075
Child aged 18 +	£1,541

Single Parent Addition Single students with dependant children may qualify for this additional allowance of £954. It cannot be paid to students who receive an Older Students' Allowance but the Single Parent Addition is paid at a higher rate, regardless of your age at the start of the course.

Initial Expenses Allowance This is a one-off payment of £55 made at the start of your course.

Practice Placement Costs These have the same rules as practice placement costs for means-tested bursary holders.

Disabled Students' Allowances These operate under the same rules as DSAs for means-tested bursary holders.

Other Funding for Diploma-level Students

Students in receipt of non-means-tested bursaries are not currently eligible to apply for student loans, although they can apply for additional assistance from the Hardship/Access to Learning Funds through their university or college. Students with children can apply for benefits and/or tax credits (more information on these can be found in Chapter 6). Diploma students who have childcare costs may also be able to apply to certain charitable trusts for assistance. You can get more details on these trusts from your university or students' union.

Students Who Will Study in Wales

Applications for funding are dealt with by the NHS (Wales) Student Awards Unit in Cardiff (details can be found in Appendix A). The arrangements for healthcare students in Wales are broadly the same as for those in England with the exception that students on degree-level nursing courses are eligible for non-means-tested bursaries, rather than means-tested bursaries. Students who receive means-tested bursaries can also apply to their LEA for a reduced-rate student loan and to their university for additional support from the Financial Contingency Funds, the Welsh equivalent of Hardship or Access to Learning Funds. If you receive a non-means-tested bursary, check with your university or college to see if you are eligible for additional assistance from the Financial Contingency Fund.

Students Who Will Study in Scotland

Most courses in Scotland lead to a degree but if you will be following a nursing course in Scotland that does not lead to a degree contact:

National Board for Nursing, Midwifery and Health Visiting for Scotland
22 Queen Street
Edinburgh
EH2 1NT
Tel: 0131 225 2096
Website: www.nbs.org.uk

If your course does lead to a degree, you can apply to the Student Awards Agency for Scotland (SAAS) for support under the Scottish Executive Health Department Bursary scheme (contact details can be found in Appendix A). Under current rules, tuition for students on these courses is free so the application to SAAS is for support with living costs.

Means-tested Maintenance Grant You can apply for a means-tested maintenance grant towards your living costs. As the name suggests, the amount you get will depend on your, your parents' or your partner's income and it does not have to be repaid. There are two different rates depending on whether you live in halls of residence/rented accommodation or in your parents' home.

Scottish Executive Health Dept Bursary Rate	Amount per year 2003/04 rates)
London rate	£2,610
Elsewhere rate	£2,115
Parental Home rate	£1,615

If you need to attend your course for more than 30 weeks and 3 days, you may get extra payments as follows:

- £92 per week if you are living away from home and studying in London
- £69 per week if you receive the 'elsewhere' rate
- £42 per week if you receive the parental home rate

Student Loan The student loan for healthcare students in Scotland is not means-tested so the amount you get does not depend on your, your parents' or your partner's income. Different rates are paid depending on whether you will be living with your parents or in halls or rented accommodation and are the same as for healthcare students in England and Wales.

Dependants' Grants If you have children or other adults who are financially dependent upon you, you may be eligible for a Dependants' Grant. The amount you receive depends on the age of the dependants and the number of dependants you have. The grants are fully means-tested so if your dependants have their own sources of income, the amount of grant you receive may be reduced. The maximum rates payable are the same as for the Dependants' Grants paid to students on other courses as shown in Chapter 3.

School Meals Grant If you receive a Dependants' Grant for children aged between 3 and 16, you will also receive a School Meals Grant. More details can be found in Chapter 3.

Lone Parents' Grant If you are bringing up children and are widowed, divorced, single or separated, you may qualify for an additional grant of £1,125.

Childcare Support for Lone Parents If you receive the Lone Parents' Grant and need to pay for formal childcare such as a registered childminder or nursery, you may qualify for additional childcare support. The amount you get will depend on the actual cost of the childcare used, but the absolute maximum grant payable is £1,050 per year at current rates.

Two Homes Grant If you need to pay a mortgage or rent to a local council or housing association for a home in addition to the home you will live in whilst studying, you may qualify for this additional grant of £795.

Travelling Expenses You can claim travelling expenses for your daily travel costs, provided they are higher than £80 per year. SAAS will pay for only the most economical method of travel, and if you are eligible for student discounts you will be expected to use them. Keep receipts and tickets as if you do not have them you will not get the money back! If you live away from your parents' home whilst studying, you can also claim for the cost of one visit home per term. There are limits on the amounts that will be covered, and air fares will only be paid if your home is on one of the offshore islands such as Orkney, Shetland or the Western Isles.

Disabled Students' Allowances If you are disabled you may qualify for a Disabled Students' Allowance as outlined in Chapter 3.

How Do I Apply?

All applications are handled by SAAS. Their contact details are in Appendix A.

How Will I Be Paid?

Bursaries are paid monthly by credit transfer to a bank account. The first instalment will cover the first two months of study.

Students Who Will Study in Northern Ireland

If you meet the eligibility conditions outlined in Chapter 1, you will be eligible for a bursary and free tuition, under the current rules. If you are from another European Union country and have been living in the EU for at least three years prior to starting your course, you will be entitled to free tuition but not a bursary for living costs.

Bursaries

If your course is in nursing, midwifery, physiotherapy, occupational therapy, radiography, speech and language therapy, podiatry or dietetics, you may be eligible for a means-tested bursary. The amount of bursary you can get will depend on your own or your family's income and there is a higher rate of bursary if you will not be living with your parents whilst studying.

Northern Ireland Healthcare Bursary Rate	Amount per year (2003/04 rates)
Away from Home rate	£2,040
Parental Home rate	£1,665

Student Loans In addition to the bursary, you might be eligible for a non-means-tested loan towards your living costs. As with all student loans, there is a lower amount available if you are in your final year of study and if you live with your parents whilst studying.

Student Loan Rates for Northern Ireland Healthcare Bursary (Final year rates are in brackets)	
Elsewhere rate	£1,960 (£1,430)
Parental Home rate	£1,500 (£1,100)

Additional Allowances You may be entitled to additional grants if you have dependants or a disability. Your ELB will be able to give you more information.

How Do I Apply?

Applications for bursary funding are dealt with by the Education and Library Board (ELB) where you live, on behalf of the Department of Health, Social Services and Public Safety. If you are from England, Wales, Scotland or another European Union country, you should apply to the North Eastern Education and Library Board (contact details can be found in Appendix A).

How Will I Be Paid?

If you are entitled to a bursary, this will be paid monthly. If you receive a student loan, it will be paid in three instalments, one at the beginning of each term.

Is That All!? 6

Funding from Other Sources

In this chapter, we will look at other funding you may be able to apply for before you start your course, whether it be from statutory (Government) sources or other sources, such as charitable trusts.

PART I – STATUTORY SOURCES

Unlike student support, which is run by devolved administrations, most other statutory funding, such as benefits and tax credits, is still the responsibility of the UK Government. This means that, generally speaking, one set of rules applies across the United Kingdom, making the system much easier to explain to you, the reader! In this section, you may come across some unfamiliar terms – these are listed below.

Terms Used

DWP – Department for Work and Pensions, responsible for the benefits system in England, Wales and Scotland

DSD – Department for Social Development, the Northern Ireland equivalent of DWP

The Revenue – the Inland Revenue, responsible for UK-wide taxation and tax credits

Jobcentre Plus – formerly the Employment Service Jobcentres and Benefits Agency offices

IS – Income Support

IBJSA – Income-Based Jobseekers' Allowance
CBJSA – Contribution-Based Jobseekers' Allowance
HB – Housing Benefit
CTB – Council Tax Benefit
DLA – Disability Living Allowance

State Benefits

Most full-time students are unable to claim state means-tested benefits. There are, however, some important exceptions but the rules differ depending on the benefit being claimed. Part-time students can claim means-tested benefits provided they meet the general eligibility criteria for the benefit concerned. You should be aware that the rules governing the benefits system are incredibly complex and in a constant state of change. What follows here is a brief outline of the benefits and which groups of students can claim. For more information, you are strongly advised to speak to a welfare officer or student adviser at your students' union or university, or your local Citizens' Advice Bureau or independent advice centre.

Income Support

What is it?

A benefit that 'tops up' the income of people on very low incomes. It is usually paid weekly and can currently be paid by 'order book' which is cashed at the Post Office, or by BACS transfer into a bank account.

Which Students Can Claim it?

The following groups of full-time students can claim Income Support:

- Lone parents of children under the age of 16 (this also includes foster parents)
- Disabled students who qualify for the disability premium; who have been incapable of work for at least 28 weeks or who qualify for DSA because of deafness
- Pensioners
- Refugees learning English, in certain circumstances

If you and your partner are both full-time students and at least one of you is responsible for a child, you can claim Income Support during the summer vacation only, as long as you fit into one of the groups who can claim Income Support.

Part-time students who meet the general conditions for Income Support can also claim.

How Do I Apply?

You claim on a Form A1 (pensioners use a Form MIG1) which you can get from your local Jobcentre Plus or Social Security office. The form is very long, approximately 45 pages, and complex. You send the form to the local Income Support office in the prepaid envelope that comes with the form and they will write to you with their decision.

How Much Will I Get?

The amount of benefit you get will depend on your family circumstances, your income and the income of any other adults who normally live with you. Entitlement to IS is worked out by calculating your income – and there are very complicated rules on how student loans and other student support funding are treated – and then by comparing your income to something known as an 'Applicable Amount'. The Applicable Amount is worked out by adding up allowances and premiums for which you qualify. For example, a single parent with one child would, under the current rules, qualify for a personal allowance, allowance for a child and a family premium. If the Applicable Amount figure is higher than your income, you get the difference paid to you as Income Support. If your income exceeds your Applicable Amount, you do not qualify for IS.

To find out if you qualify for IS and to see how much you might get, contact a welfare officer or student adviser at your university. Most advisers are able to do IS calculations so will be able to tell you if you are likely to get anything. Many students will not qualify for IS during term time as the student loan is taken into account as income. However, it is ignored during the long summer vacation which, for benefit purposes, is taken to be July and August, so single parents especially may qualify for IS during the summer vacation.

WARNING!

2003/2004 is a transitional year for IS due to the introduction of the new tax credits system. There will be major changes to IS from April 2004 but exact details were not available at the time of writing.

Jobseekers' Allowance

What is it?

A benefit paid to those who are out of work but actively seeking work. For this reason, most full-time students are excluded. The two exceptions are:

- Student couples responsible for at least one child. This applies only during the summer vacation and only if you are available for and actively seeking work.
- Students who have taken time out of their studies, with the agreement of the university, because of caring responsibilities or illness. That caring responsibility or illness must have come to an end and you must be waiting to return to your course.

Part-time students can claim JSA if they meet the 'labour market conditions' which means you must be available for work, actively seeking work and have signed a jobseeker's agreement with Jobcentre Plus.

How Do I Apply?

You need to attend an interview with an adviser at your local Jobcentre Plus. Once you have signed a jobseeker's agreement, you need to attend the Jobcentre Plus every two weeks in order to 'sign on'. Each time you visit the office, you need to show that you have been looking for work and keep a diary of your jobseeking activities. If they are not satisfied, your benefit may be stopped.

How is it Paid?

Usually by BACS transfer to a bank account every two weeks.

Housing Benefit

What is it?

Housing Benefit (HB) can help pay your rent if you are on a low income. It is means-tested and administered by local councils – not necessarily the same people as your LEA. Once again, most full-time students are not entitled to claim Housing Benefit as, somewhat bizarrely, the regulations state that full-time students are not treated as liable to pay rent! However, some groups of full-time students can claim Housing Benefit:

● Students receiving IS or IBJSA
● Lone parents
● Student couples who are responsible for at least one child (unlike IS, this applies all year round)
● Pensioners
● Disabled students who qualify for disability premium; have been incapable of work for at least 28 weeks or who qualify for DSA because they are deaf
● Students who have taken time out of their studies, with the agreement of the university, because of caring responsibilities or illness. That caring responsibility or illness must have come to an end and you must be waiting to return to your course.

Once again, part-time students who satisfy the general qualifying conditions for Housing Benefit may be eligible. Students who live in accommodation rented from their university are not eligible for Housing Benefit.

How Do I Apply?

If you have applied for Income Support, the claim pack will have included a claim form for Housing Benefit. However, most councils will ask for an application to be made on their own application form. They will also ask for supporting documentation, which will include evidence of your income and income of any dependants, and other adults who may be living with you. They will also need to see proof of the rent that you pay and may ask for confirmation from the landlord that you are actually his or her tenant. Different councils apply the rules in different ways so you are best advised to check with your council exactly what evidence they might require. The council is supposed to deal with the claim within four weeks of it being submitted, and payments are supposed to start from the Monday after they receive the form. In practice, however, many councils take much longer than four weeks to process claims for HB, which can result in hardship and landlords beginning proceedings for eviction. If this happens to you, contact a welfare officer or student adviser immediately.

How Much Will I Get?

Housing Benefit is means-tested so the amount you get will depend on the amount of rent you actually pay, your income and your 'Applicable Amount' as for Income Support. Unlike Income Support, however, if your income exceeds your Applicable Amount you may still get some Housing Benefit. Many student parents receive HB all year round so it is worth applying!

WARNING!

Many councils will tell you that because you are a full-time student you will not get any Housing Benefit. Whilst this is true in most cases, if you are studying full-time and are in one of the groups listed above, you may still get some Housing Benefit. Insist that they give you a claim form!

How is it Paid?

The payment method will depend on who your landlord is. If you rent from the council, Housing Benefit may be known as a 'Rent Rebate' and your benefit will be transferred to your rent account, leaving you to pay any outstanding balance. If you rent your home from a social landlord, such as a Housing Association, the council may be able to make direct payments to them on your behalf. If you rent privately, the council may send you a cheque or pay you by BACS directly into your bank account.

Council Tax Benefit

What is it?

A benefit, administered by the local council, that can help towards payment of your Council Tax bill. Only certain groups of students are able to apply for Council Tax Benefit, and these groups are the same as for Housing Benefit. However, if only full-time students live in your home then you should apply for Council Tax Exemption – for more information, see Chapter 10.

How Do I Apply?

Contact your local council for an application form. If you are applying for Housing Benefit, the form may also include an application for Council Tax Benefit as the two benefits operate under similar rules.

How is it Paid?

The council will pay the benefit direct to your Council Tax account and send you a new bill showing the benefit payments and the reduced amount, if any, that you have to pay.

Disability Living Allowance

What is it?

A benefit for people who need help getting around, or who have care or supervision needs. It has two components – mobility and care – and they can be paid at a number of rates depending on the severity of the disability. As it is a non-means-tested benefit, it is not affected by any student support income you have, nor is it affected by the mere fact that you may be studying.

How Do I Apply?

You need to contact the Benefits Information Line on 0800 88 22 00 or send back a reply card for a dated application form. The application form is very complicated and is in two separate parts. Forms need to be sent to a central processing centre – a prepaid envelope is enclosed with the application form.

How is it Paid?

DLA is usually paid every four weeks, either by Order Book or by BACS transfer into your bank account.

WARNING!

The rules on Disability Living Allowance and the application form are incredibly complicated. Your university disability adviser, welfare officer or student adviser may be able to help with any queries you have. In addition, SKILL may be able to give you some information. Their contact details can be found in Appendix B.

Carers' Allowance

What is it?

A benefit paid to people who provide substantial care for a person who receives higher or middle-rate care component of DLA (or Attendance Allowance, which is the equivalent of DLA for people over 65). It is not means-tested but is unavailable to people in full-time employment or full-time education. Unfortunately, full-time education is not properly defined so it has been left open to interpretation by the courts. Until recently, advisers thought that the requirements of full-time education would refer only to time spent in lectures or tutorials or other 'contact' time. However, the Court of Appeal has recently decided that 'supervised study', which is the terminology used in the regulations, also applies to time spent working away from university premises on course-related material. This, in effect, means that no full-time student can claim Carers' Allowance, even if they are engaged in full-time care as well as study. The decision does not, however, affect part-time students.

How do I Apply?

Carers' Allowance is dealt with by a central DWP office in Preston, Lancashire.

How is it Paid?

Carers' Allowance is usually paid either by Order Book or by BACS transfer direct to your bank account.

This is not the whole list of benefits that may be available but they are the main ones students can access. For further information contact your university's welfare service, students' union or your local CAB or independent advice centre.

Tax Credits

The tax credits system, administered by the Inland Revenue, changed quite substantially in April 2003 when two new credits came into force – Child Tax Credit and Working Tax Credit. From April 2004, there will be further changes as some of the support for children currently paid through Income Support or Income-based Jobseekers' Allowance will be paid through the tax credits system. Tax credits also replace Dependants' Allowances for Children for students from England, Wales and Northern Ireland from September 2003 (and probably Scotland from September 2004) so you need to know about the system and how to apply. Married students with children will qualify for some parts of the tax credits provided the total family income does not exceed £58,000 per year.

What Are They?

Tax credits provide additional support to families with children, employed people over the age of 25 on low incomes and disabled workers.

Working Tax Credit provides additional support to:

- Single parents who work at least 16 hours per week
- Couples with children, where one member of the couple works at least 16 hours per week
- Disabled people who work at least 16 hours per week
- Single people aged over 25 who work at least 30 hours per week

To qualify, you must be in work or have an offer of a job that will start within seven days of you submitting the claim. The work must be due to continue for at least four weeks. This means that students aged 25 or over who work at least 30 hours per week for at least four weeks of the long summer vacation can claim Working Tax Credit. Similarly, this group of students can also claim WTC for any placement year, provided they are working at least 30 hours per week.

Like Child Tax Credit, the Working Tax Credit is made up of a number of elements – a basic element for working with additions if you are either a lone parent or part of a couple; if you work more than 30 hours per week; if you have a disability or if you are aged over 50 and are starting work having been out of work for at least three months. There is also a childcare element that can cover 70% of eligible childcare costs (which are the same as for

Childcare Grants as outlined in Chapter 2) but, if you are part of a couple, both of you must be working in order to claim this.

Child Tax Credit provides additional support for families with children. You do not have to be in work to be able to receive the Child Tax Credit. It is made up of a number of elements – everyone with at least one child gets a basic Family Element of approximately £10.45 per week, provided their income is below £50,000. This element is doubled if there is a child under one year old in the family. You also get an element for each child, which is higher if the child is either disabled or severely disabled. Most student parents will qualify for some or all of the Child Tax Credit. Unlike the benefits system, student loans are not included as income in the means test for tax credits. In fact, at the time of writing, it was understood that the only student income that would be taken into account from September 2003 would be Dependants' Allowances for Children paid to students from Scotland (but not Dependants' Allowances paid under the NHS Bursary scheme) and any element of a Career Development Loan paid for living costs. For single-parent students, this means that weekly amounts of Child Tax Credit could be as shown in the table below.

Estimated Maximum Weekly Child Tax Credit Entitlement for a Single-parent Student (from April 2003 to April 2004)	
With 1 child	£38.28
With 2 children	£66.09
With 3 children	£93.89
With 4 children	£121.69

(This example assumes that the single student has no other income, none of the children are aged under one and none of the children are disabled.)

How Do I Apply?

You can claim tax credits by filling in a form (Form TC600), which you can get from your local Inland Revenue Enquiry Centre, by telephoning 0800 500 222 or from Jobcentre Plus. Some student services departments and students' unions also have copies – it is worth asking. You can also apply online via the Inland Revenue secure website at www.inlandrevenue.gov.uk/taxcredits

The Revenue are also operating a helpline to answer queries. Their contact details can be found in Appendix A.

How is it Paid?

If you are entitled to Working Tax Credit and Child Tax Credit, any element of Working Tax Credit will be paid through payroll by an employer. Child Tax Credit and any childcare element of WTC will be paid direct to the person with main caring responsibility for the children by the Inland Revenue via BACS transfer. Payments via pay-roll will be paid at the same frequency as your pay, usually monthly. Direct payments from the Inland Revenue can be paid either weekly or four-weekly – you can choose and specify which you prefer on your application form.

PART II – OTHER SOURCES

We have already looked at funding that comes from statutory, or Government, sources. This is funding to which, depending on your circumstances, you have a statutory entitlement. However, there are some other sources of funding or raising money to help pay for your studies that you could consider. Funding that you can apply for before you start your course is outlined here, but your university may also have funds that you can apply for once you have started your course. These funds are outlined in Chapter 13.

Savings

As you will see from Section 4 of this book, the student loan on its own is not usually enough to support you throughout the full academic year. You are therefore likely to need money from other sources to keep you going. Whilst savings will not be an option for everybody, they can be a useful safety net in case of money problems. You may be able to put some money into a savings account if you have taken a gap year before going to university, or have worked during the summer before starting your course.

A savings account can also be useful to help with budgeting. Remember that your student loan will normally be paid in termly instalments. If you have budgeted properly (see Chapter 12) you may find it useful to put some of your term's loan payment into a savings account so that it is earning interest, and only withdraw it towards the end of the term when you know you will need it.

Savings – Pros and Cons

PROS	CONS
Can be a useful safety net	Some banks require £500 to open an account and a minimum balance to be kept in the account
Can help with budgeting	
You earn interest	
If you use an account that does not have a cash card, your access to the money is controlled/limited	It may not be possible to save enough to plug the shortfall of the student loan
You can put money aside from work during the vacations for use during term time	You may need to give notice to access your money

Parents or Family

It is estimated that about one-third of undergraduate students in England and Wales have an assessed parental or family contribution towards their living costs. This happens when family income is above £31,230 for students who are assessed as dependent on their parents by the LEA. In this case, the parental contribution replaces part of the means-tested student loan, as we saw in earlier chapters. However, even if there is no assessed contribution, some parents or other family members may be willing and able to help. This might be in the form of a loan or them paying your rent for you. Or it may be helping you out with a box of groceries if they come to visit or you visit them. Some families are able to give a weekly or monthly allowance. Whether large or small, do not underestimate the help that support from your parents can give you. Having said that, your parents may not be willing to keep dipping into their pockets every couple of weeks so think carefully before you ask for extra help, especially if they are already providing regular financial assistance.

Family Contributions – Pros and Cons

PROS	CONS
Can be a useful safety net	May not be able or willing to meet all your requests for help
Can provide help when you need it most	More than one member of the family at university can be a very heavy strain on the family finances
Might help by paying for your accommodation or by providing a regular allowance	
	If you fall out with your parents they may stop helping

Sponsorship, Scholarships and Bursaries

If you have been working before starting your course, it may be worth asking your employer if they would be willing to sponsor you whilst at university. In some cases, if the course is relevant to the work you have been doing, employers may help by contributing towards tuition fees, living costs or both. This is usually more relevant to postgraduate study but if you have been working for a company for some time and they can see clear career development prospects from your course, they might just be willing to help.

There are also some scholarships and bursaries available to undergraduate students – some from universities and some from other sources. It is worth asking your university if they offer any scholarships and, if they do, what criteria you need to meet in order to qualify for one. In some cases, you may need an academic reference from your current school or college, or you may need to live in a certain area targeted by the university. Different schemes have different rules but remember that funding is not guaranteed and not all universities offer scholarship or bursary schemes. A good source of information on scholarships and bursaries is the website www. scholarship-search.org.uk

Sponsorship, Scholarships and Bursaries – Pros and Cons	
PROS	CONS
Can provide useful additional money	Conditions may be attached to employer sponsorship, e.g. you have to agree to work for them for a number of years after graduation
Can be used to pay for fees or provide living costs (depending on rules of the scheme)	
	Lots of competition

Part-time Work

Many students supplement their income by working. This may be one or two evenings a week, at the weekend or during the vacations. However, part-time employment may not be an option for some students. For example, nursing and midwifery students often have to work shifts as part of the practical experience requirement of their courses. Engineering and science students often have to undertake laboratory work in addition to lectures, seminars and tutorials. Once you start your course, you will soon be able to work out whether part-time employment is appropriate or, indeed, possible.

SEE ALSO
Chapter 13 – part-time work, income tax and the National Minimum Wage

Charitable Trusts

A number of educational trusts and charities can provide invaluable additional funding to help with studying at university. Criteria of the various charities vary enormously. In some cases, you must have been living in a particular parish, attending a certain church or living within a certain radius of a particular village, church or even house. Some charities will only support students on certain courses, and others will only support students if their parents are or were engaged in certain occupations. Your university student services department or students' union may have information on particular charitable trusts that accept applications from students. Alternatively, your university library may have copies of books such as the *Educational Grants Directory* or *A Guide to Grants for Individuals in Need* (both published by Directory of Social Change) which have lists of charities, tell you who is eligible to apply and how to make an application. In some cases, they also give an indication of the level of awards made by the trusts. Your students' union or student services department may have a computer program called *FunderFinder* which can identify trusts whose criteria you seem to meet. One thing you will notice very quickly is that awards tend to be quite small, sometimes in the region of £250. You should not, therefore, rely on trust funding except as a 'top up' to other sources of funding.

Many trusts receive more applications than they can support so it is therefore important to target any application in order to maximise your chances of success. If you have done your research well, you will have identified trusts for which you meet the eligibility criteria and found out whether you need an application form or whether you need to write a letter to apply. In some cases, a third party will need to apply on your behalf – this could be your university's welfare service or students' union. If a trust states that it can only provide grants of, say, £500, it is really not worth applying if you are asking for £4,000. Some trusts will appreciate a budget plan, showing the shortfall you are asking them to assist with meeting. They may also want to know where else you have applied for funds, in particular that you have exhausted all sources of statutory funding available to you.

SEE ALSO
Chapter 8 – banking
Chapter 12 – discretionary funds
Educational Grants Advisory Service – Contact details in Appendix B

But What About Me?

Funding for Part-time Students and Students from Outside the UK

If you will be studying part-time or are from another European Union country, certain offshore islands or overseas, this chapter contains information for you. Funding for these groups is somewhat different to those from the UK studying full-time.

Part-time Study

If you decide to study a part-time undergraduate degree and have a low enough income, you may qualify for additional support. The system in England and Wales will be changing from September 2004 so you will find outlined below the current system of financial support and the changes that will come into force. One thing common to all sources of funding is the residency requirement. You must have been 'ordinarily resident' in the UK for at least three years before the start of your course and there must be no restriction on your stay. For more information on the residency requirement, please see Chapter 1.

Tuition Fees

At present, students apply to their university for help with tuition fees. This is known as 'fee waiver'. There are a number of further conditions, in addition to the residency requirement, in order to qualify for fee waiver.

Fee Waiver

- You must meet the residency condition (see Chapter 1)
- Your course must be at least 50% of the full-time equivalent (60 credit points per year) or 25% of the full-time equivalent (30 credit points per year) if you have a disability
- You must have a low income
- You must not already hold a degree-level award

Your course You must usually be studying at least 50% of the full-time equivalent course in order to qualify for fee waiver. The exception to this rule is for disabled students who can be studying 25% of the full-time course and qualify. An academic year of a full-time course is normally 120 credit points, so to qualify for fee waiver you need to be studying 60 credits (30 credits if disabled) in the academic year.

Your income You must have a low income. In 2003/04, for a single person, the income threshold is £14,200.

Previous Study If you already have a degree or equivalent you will not usually be eligible for a fee waiver. The exception to this rule is if you finished your degree a long time ago and are doing the new course in order to retrain for a new career and improve your employment prospects.

How Do I Apply?

Fee waivers are administered by your university, usually by the student services department. They will need to see evidence of your income and of the number of credit points you will be studying in that academic year. Different universities have different application procedures so you should check with your university.

How is it Paid?

If your application is agreed, the full amount of your tuition fees will be paid on your behalf.

Student Loans

Part-time students can apply to their LEA for a student loan of £500, regardless of where they will be studying. The application forms are different to those used by full-time students and can be obtained from the LEA, the DfES Student Support Information Line (details in Appendix A) or in some cases from your university. Once again, you need to meet the residency requirement as outlined in Chapter 1 and you must also be aged under 54. If you are aged between 51 and 54, you will need to sign a declaration that you intend to seek full-time paid employment after finishing your course. This is because the student loan is repaid through the income tax system. Your university will need to confirm your attendance on the course and, like the fee waiver, you need to be studying at least 50% of the full-time course. You also need to be on a low income, but the threshold is different to that for fee waiver. If you have dependants, the threshold is raised.

How Do I Apply?

When you have filled in the form, return it to your LEA. Unlike loans for full-time students, you apply for a student loan for part-time study once you have started your course. The loan application pack includes the application to the LEA and the loan request form. If the LEA decides you are eligible for the loan they will send your loan request to the Student Loans Company.

How is it Paid?

The student loan for part-time students is paid by BACS transfer, directly to your bank account, in one lump sum. Payment is usually made 28 days after the application is agreed.

Changes from September 2004

The following changes to part-time support come into force in September 2004:

- Fee waiver will be replaced with a grant for tuition fees, administered by the LEA. You will still need to be studying 50% of the full-time course and have a low income. The income threshold will, however, be higher than for part-time fee waiver.
- Student loans will be replaced with means-tested grants of £250, administered by the LEA. Once again, you will need to have a low income.
- Students studying at least 10% (12 credits) of the full-time equivalent will be able to apply to their university for a discretionary fee waiver.

Other Funding Available to Part-time Students

Part-time students can access other sources of funding. Details of most of these can be found in Chapter 6.

- State benefits to certain groups, especially lone parents and disabled students. However, any part-time student can claim Jobseekers' Allowance, provided their attendance on the course does not 'unreasonably restrict' their availability for work.
- Tax credits – Working Tax Credit for students with children, if working more than 16 hours per week, or disabled students who work more than 16 hours per week, or single students aged 25 or over who work more than 30 hours per week. Child Tax Credit for any students with children.
- Trusts and charities, although some will only support students who are studying full-time.
- Hardship funds (or equivalent) from your university (see Chapter 12).

Students from Offshore Islands

Students from the Channel Islands or the Isle of Man are not eligible for student loans or any other student funding from the UK Government. Instead, the relevant Island authorities (States of Jersey, States of Guernsey and Isle of Man Government) operate their own student support schemes. Many students from these islands can receive maintenance grants whilst studying in the UK. To find out exactly what is available, contact your Island authority – their contact details can be found in Appendix A.

European Union Students

European Union Countries (excluding the UK)		
Austria	Germany	Netherlands
Belgium	Greece	Portugal
Denmark	Ireland	Spain
Finland	Italy	Sweden
France	Luxembourg	

If you are a national of one of the countries listed in the above table, you may qualify for assistance with your tuition fees. You will need to be able to prove that you have been resident in that country for at least three years prior to starting your course. You will not, however, be able to apply for a student loan or other funding for living costs available from the UK Government. If your country becomes a member of the European Union whilst you are studying, you may qualify for assistance with your tuition fees, from the next academic year, provided you meet all the other eligibility criteria.

How Do I Apply?

Applications from EU students who will be studying in England and Wales are dealt with by the European Team of the Department for Education and Skills (Appendix A). Any assistance with tuition fees will be means-tested in the same way as for students from the UK.

If you will be studying in Scotland contact the Student Awards Agency for Scotland. If you will be studying in Northern Ireland contact the relevant Education and Library Board. See Appendix A for details.

How is it Paid?

If you are eligible to receive assistance with your tuition fees, any contribution from the UK Government will be paid direct to your university. If this does not cover the full amount of your tuition fees, you will need to pay the balance to your university yourself.

Overseas Students

Students from countries outside the European Union will usually have a stamp in their passports stating that they have no recourse to public funds and that any work must be authorised. This means that you cannot apply for any student support funding, all of which is provided by the UK Government, nor can you claim any state benefits or tax credits. However, your university may offer some bursaries or scholarships specifically for overseas (usually known as international) students, so it is worth asking the International Students Adviser, if your university has one, or the Admissions Office at your university if any funding is available for overseas students.

The good news is that, provided your passport is not stamped with a *prohibition* on work, you can work up to 20 hours per week during term time and unlimited hours during vacations.

SEE ALSO
Chapter 12 – part-time work

Banking and Credit

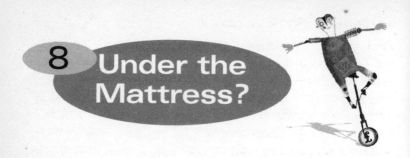

8 Under the Mattress?

Now that you know what money you should have coming in, you need somewhere to put it. Will it all go under your mattress? In a piggy bank? Or into a bank account? Of course, as most people will know, a bank account is the most sensible option if you want your cash to be stored safely, easily accessed and even earning a bit of interest for you. Throughout this section, 'bank account' is used to refer to an account held at a bank or a building society.

Why Should I Have a Bank Account?

Well, to start off with, if you don't have a bank account, you will have no way of receiving your student loan. Most students will receive their first instalments via BACS (or electronic funds transfer), and all second and third instalments are paid by BACS. If you are doing a nursing, midwifery or other health-profession course, your bursary from the NHS will also be paid by BACS. So as you can see, if you do not have an account you will have no way of receiving your money. But that is not the only reason why you need a bank account. Remember, under current rules, the student loan is paid in three instalments. One instalment of the loan could be up to £1,700, depending on the amount you get and whether or not you study in London. That part of the loan may be paid in, say, mid-September, when you first start your course. Your next instalment will be paid after Christmas at the beginning of the second term in January. It does not take a genius to work out that careful budgeting will be necessary. This is where a bank account can come in very useful.

Opening a Bank Account

Each summer, the main banks advertise the details of their student services for students starting courses that year. They may try to entice you with hard cash, or a mobile phone, DVD player or even a toaster. Nice, you might think – £50 cash at the start of your course will come in very handy. So will that nice gleaming toaster – especially for all the beans on toast you are likely to be eating over the next few years. But what are they *really* offering? Look at these comparisons of three (fictitious) banks:

Comparing Bank Accounts

BANK A	BANK B	BANK C
£50 cash when account opened	Toaster, kettle and CD player	No gimmicks
Free use of all UK cash machines	£1.50 charge for using non-Bank B cash machines	Free use of all UK and Ireland cash machines
Internet banking	0.2% APR interest if in credit	Internet and telephone banking
2% APR interest if in credit	Interest-free overdraft negotiable	3% credit interest rate
Up to £1,000 interest-free overdraft	19.9% unauthorised overdraft fee	Up to £1,500 interest-free over-draft in year 1 rising to £3,000 in year 3
33% unauthorised overdraft fee	Nearest branch 10 miles away from campus	14.9% unauthorised overdraft rate
Branch on campus		Branch in town nearest campus

So which one offers the best deal? That depends on how you use the account. If your nearest branch of Bank B is 10 miles away but you will be using cash machines regularly, Bank B may not be the best deal for you, as they charge for cash machine transactions from machines owned by other banks. However, if you budget carefully but know that towards the end of each term, or perhaps more often, you will need to use an overdraft, a low overdraft interest rate and higher credit interest rate will be of more use, so Bank C would be most appropriate. Whichever applies to you, these tips should help you make a decision when opening an account.

Top Tips – Opening a Bank Account

Ask the following questions:

- Is there a branch on or near my university campus?
- Where is the nearest cash machine?
- Do I get charged for using other banks' cash machines?
- Can I get an overdraft?
- Will I be charged for using an overdraft? And if so, how much?
- Do I get a cheque book?
- Do I get a debit card?
- Is telephone/internet/mobile phone banking available?
- How much interest do I get paid if my account is in credit?
- What other services do I get?
- After I finish my course, how long does the preferential service continue?
- When you have decided on the right account for you, make sure you open it before starting your course.

Parents Pay Attention! – How You Can Help

A bank account is *essential* for your daughter or son to receive their student loan or NHS Bursary. You can help by making sure they have opened an account and know their bank details at least one month (preferably earlier) before starting their course.

Banking Facilities

So now you have opened a bank account, what have you actually got? Facilities offered by the various banks will differ but most student current accounts will include some or all of the following:

ATM Card or Cash Card. A card that allows you to withdraw cash from a 'hole in the wall' cash machine, sometimes known as an ATM ('Automatic Teller Machine'). These are usually sited at banks but are becoming more common in other locations such as shopping centres, railway stations and university campuses. They usually work with a four-digit PIN or Personal Identification Number that the bank will send you.

BACS Payments can be made into most bank accounts. Student loans are paid in by BACS as are wages or salary from most employers.

Cheque Books allow you to pay money to someone else. You write the cheque and the person receiving it pays it into their bank account. Your account is then debited.

How to Write a Cheque

Andrew needs to pay £200 to the University of Chipping Sodbury to pay the deposit for his halls fees for the year. He needs to put the following in the following places:

❶ Today's date
❷ University of Chipping Sodbury
❸ Two hundred pounds only
❹ 200.00
❺ His signature

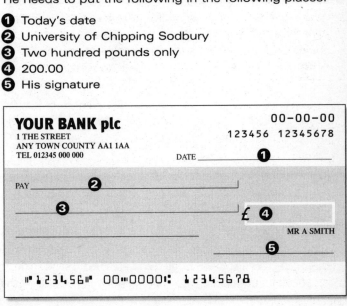

The completed cheque looks like this:

YOUR BANK plc
1 THE STREET
ANY TOWN COUNTY AA1 1AA
TEL 012345 000 000

00-00-00
123456 12345678

DATE 1st October 2003

PAY University of Chipping Sodbury

Two hundred pounds only

£ 200.00

MR A SMITH
Andrew Smith

⑈123456⑈ 00⑈0000⑇ 12345678

Many students are unsure how to complete a cheque – mainly because they rarely use them. Now you have no excuse!

Cheque Guarantee Card. A cheque guarantee card can be used to 'guarantee' payment of a cheque. If you pay by cheque for goods in a shop you will be asked for a guarantee card, and if you do not have one you will probably be asked to use another form of payment. The retailer will write the card number on the back of the cheque, and payment of that cheque is then 'guaranteed' meaning that, provided the value of the cheque is below the limit of the card, the bank will honour the cheque. Although this is an old-fashioned way of making payments, some people do still use it.

Debit Card These commonly have a Switch, Solo or Maestro logo, or Visa or Electron from some banks. If you have a debit card, and most current accounts include a debit card, it will be a combined cash, cheque guarantee and debit card. When you pay by debit card, the retailer will swipe the card through the till or payment terminal and enter the amount. You then sign a receipt and the money is debited from your account. Some newer cards contain a smart chip. If your card has one of these, the retailer will insert the card into their payment terminal and ask you to enter your PIN number. The money will then be debited from your account, so you need to make sure there is enough money in the account to cover the payment! In many ways, debit cards are paperless cheques, except that the money comes out of your account quicker than if paying by cheque.

Standing Order If you need to make a regular payment of a regular amount to someone else, a standing order is the easiest way to do this. You tell your bank the amount you want to pay, the date, and the sort code, account number and reference of the person or company you will be paying. They will then debit this amount from your account on the dates instructed by you until you tell them otherwise. Standing orders can be useful for paying some bills, putting money into a savings account or paying money to friends and family.

Direct Debit is another method that can be used to make payments to other people. It is commonly used by utility companies (gas, electricity and the like), universities for tuition fees and other companies to whom you make regular but variable payments. You sign an authority form and give it to the company who will be receiving the payments, who inform the bank of the authority. On the dates you have agreed with the company, the bank debits the agreed amount from your account. There are rules the company needs to follow if the amount you pay or the date of payment change. You will be given a copy of the main rules when you sign a direct debit form, usually called a 'mandate'.

Overdraft There are two sorts of overdraft – authorised and unauthorised. An authorised overdraft will have been agreed by the bank before it is used. An unauthorised overdraft will not have been agreed. Overdrawing your account means taking more money out of it than you have put in. For a student, an overdraft is often necessary. Most banks will let student account holders overdraw their account up to a certain amount without charging any interest, so check with your bank. Any overdrawn amount above this level will usually attract an unauthorised overdraft interest rate, which can be as high as 25% with some banks. In addition, further charges may apply whilst the account is in unauthorised overdraft, so always speak to your bank before going overdrawn.

Telephone Banking allows you to deal with certain aspects of your account over the telephone, either by an automated service or by speaking to a member of staff. Services commonly available with telephone banking are balance enquiries, details of recent transactions, paying bills, setting up and cancelling standing orders or requesting changes to your overdraft limit.

Internet Banking works in a similar way to telephone banking, except you access it via the internet.

WAP Banking Some accounts now let you access some information using a WAP-enabled mobile phone. As third-generation mobiles become more available, other services will also be available by this method.

TV Banking Some banks allow access to account details via interactive digital television. This works in a similar way to internet banking.

Your bank may offer additional services, such as commission-free foreign exchange or discounted travel or home insurance. It is always worth asking what other facilities are available.

Top Tips – Dealing with the Bank Manager

- Never exceed your overdraft limit without talking to the bank first. They are more likely to be sympathetic if you have a good reason why you need the extension, such as paying the rent, and can show that it will be temporary and you will be able to pay it back.

- Make sure the bank has your correct contact address. Confirm any changes of address straight away – many banks will now let you do this via the internet or telephone.

- Do not be afraid to talk to them! They will offer advice if, for example, you need to change to part-time study and will not be entitled to any more student loan.

- Open all letters from the bank when they arrive and keep copies of bank statements. If you deal with matters at an early stage, a later crisis can often be avoided! (See Chapter 13 for more details.)
- Confirm all telephone calls with a follow-up letter. This will protect you at a later date if there is a dispute over what has been agreed with the bank.

One final word of warning – think very carefully before opening more than one student account. Many banks will make it a condition that your student support funding is paid into that account. If you have more than one account, you can obviously pay your loan into only one of them, so the other bank may say you have breached their terms and conditions and close the account. If you have run up a large over-draft, they may decide to reclaim it immediately.

The 'Never Never', aka Credit

Many banks offer credit cards to students. Some will visit university campuses during Freshers' events, offering lots of gimmicks such as cameras or mobile phones to those who sign up. Many shops will also try to persuade you to open their store card account, often with a promise of 10% or so off all purchases in that shop for a certain period of time.

How Credit Works

You sign an agreement, known as a 'credit agreement', which allows you to borrow money from the card issuer – sometimes, but not always, a bank. They issue you with a plastic card and tell you what your 'credit limit' is. This is the maximum amount you can borrow using the card. You can then use the card to pay for goods and services and, in some cases, withdraw cash. Each month, you have to make a minimum contractual payment, which is often between 2% and 5% of the outstanding balance. If you pay the full amount owed by the date due, you pay no interest. However, if there is a balance left by the time the next statement is issued, you will pay interest on the amount outstanding. Interest rates vary between cards and can be as low as about 11% per year or as high as 30% per year on many store cards. If you do not make at least the minimum payment each month you may incur charges, which can be as much as £20 per missed payment. You therefore need to think very carefully before using a credit card and, if you do use one, make sure you are able to make at least the minimum payment each month. It is very easy to get into difficulty with credit cards if you do not keep an eye on the amount being spent on them each month. Credit card companies supply information on accounts, including whether minimum payments are made and arrears, to organisations known as Credit Reference Agencies. These agencies supply information to other banks who subscribe to their services and, if you have had difficulties making payments in the past, you might find it difficult to get more credit in future. This could mean, for example, that if you wanted to go on to postgraduate study, you might be turned down for a Career Development Loan, or if you applied for other forms of credit you might be refused.

SEE ALSO
Chapter 13 – dealing with debt

Part 3

Where Does All the Money Go?

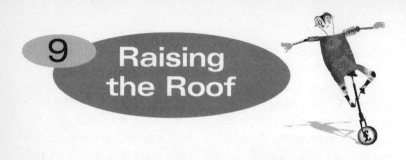

9 Raising the Roof

No – we are not talking about the noise of that party you went to last night. In this chapter, we are going to look at having a place to live – finding somewhere, paying for it, and what to do if things go wrong.

WARNING!

Housing and Landlord and Tenant law is in a constant state of change so we can only go into the very basics here. If you encounter any difficulties, you are strongly advised to seek advice from a welfare officer or student adviser in your students' union or university student services department.

What Sort of Accommodation?

When we talk about university accommodation, we are referring to the following:

- catered halls of residence
- self-catering halls of residence
- 'head-leased' properties

In addition, some private companies manage halls of residence on behalf of universities, although room allocation is usually still carried out by universities. This is becoming increasingly common across the country.

Availability of university halls accommodation is a major factor in deciding which university to go to. Many universities will attempt to guarantee places in halls for first-year students who live at least a certain distance from the university. Others will guarantee a certain number of places to postgraduate or overseas students for example, so check with your university exactly what is available.

Catered Halls

Catered halls are sometimes more expensive than self-catered halls but you usually get breakfast and an evening meal thrown in, at least during the week. That can save you quite a bit of money, even though you may pay more in rent. However, will you really be out of bed every day in time for breakfast? Will you always be there in time for dinner? If your university has more than one campus and you have to attend classes on a campus other than that where your hall is based, it may be difficult to get back in time for the evening meal, so are you really saving money by living in a catered hall? Having said that, if you know that your timetable will allow you to be back in time for meals, this may be more beneficial for you, as well as giving you the chance to meet people without being 'under the influence'!

Some students do appreciate the savings that can be made by living in a catered hall, but you do need to consider if you are going to reap the full benefit of the catering facilities before signing a Halls Licence (more on that later). If you decide to live in catered halls but never make it to breakfast or dinner, and have to pay for these meals on top of what you have already paid to live there in the first place, you will find that your student loan will not last very long. . . .

Self-catered Halls

These are usually, but not always, cheaper than catered halls. Many universities only have self-catered halls so the catered option may not be available. The name says it all – you do your own catering! These halls come with kitchens shared between a group of students, which can lead to arguments when it comes to cupboard or fridge space and cleaning up! However, they can be an excellent way of meeting people when you first go to university and let you gain your sense of independence. Of course, it helps if you can cook and cope with doing your own washing up. Cleaners in halls have been known to confiscate crockery and cutlery if it has been left unwashed for a length of time!

Having decided between catered or self-catered halls, if both options are available, you may have another choice to make – 'standard' or 'en suite'.

Standard Halls

A standard hall of residence will have one bathroom shared between a number of students. How many share the facilities varies between different halls but it can be up to six or so people sharing one bathroom. In standard halls, you usually find that there is a wash basin in each room, in addition to the shared bathrooms. Rooms in standard halls are usually cheaper than en-suite halls but remember that you may have to queue for the bath or shower or even the loo!

En-suite Halls

These usually have a bath or shower room for each study bedroom. This can make the actual room quite a bit smaller than a standard hall room, or an odd shape – especially if a standard hall has been converted and a shower room 'pod' fitted inside the original room. In addition, en-suite rooms are more expensive than rooms in standard halls. Some, but not all, universities set aside specific accommodation for mature or married students. Ask your university's accommodation office for more information.

Hall Seniors

Some universities employ students as residential wardens, tutors or 'Hall Seniors'. These students are often in their final or postgraduate year of study. Hall seniors can provide an additional safety net for first-year students living in halls. They will know the area and whom to contact if there are problems and act as a first port of call if there are any problems.

Halls of Residence – Things to Consider

- Catered or self-catering?
- Standard or en suite?
- How far away from the place of study is it?
- Is there transport between place of study and halls of residence?
- How many people will you be sharing with?
- How much is the weekly rent?
- Do you have to pay for anything extra (e.g. electricity)?

Head-leasing Schemes

Some universities operate something known as a head-leasing scheme. They rent properties from landlords in the area and 'sub-let' them to groups of students. The students have a contract with the university and pay the rent to the university. The rent is then passed on to the landlord of the property, sometimes with a management fee deducted, which is also common in the private rented sector. Head leasing has many advantages over the private rented sector, and in some respects is a 'halfway house' between halls accommodation and the private sector. However, remember the following:

- The rent in a head-leased property may be higher than in halls
- You will probably be responsible for household bills (see Chapter 10)
- The property could be some distance from the main university campus and transport links may not be all that good
- Your neighbours are likely to be local residents who may not take too kindly to having a group of students living next door to them

Having said that, a head-leased property may still be preferable to renting in the private sector as you are likely to have direct contact with your landlord, i.e. the university, in case things go wrong.

Renting through an Agent

In many areas, the main source of accommodation is letting or estate agents. Many towns with high numbers of students have specialist agents who target the student population or market certain properties as 'student lets'. On the other hand, there are some agents who will not allow students to rent from them, often because the landlords have instructed them not to accept students as tenants. Letting agents may advertise at your university on special noticeboards, and the easiest way of finding what is available is to visit the agent's office. Alternatively, you could look in the local paper – in many areas there are now free property papers – but bear in mind that these are generally aimed at working people, and rents are often higher than students can afford. Many agents now also advertise properties to let on the internet on various local websites – details of the relevant addresses can be found in your local property papers or from the agents themselves.

Private Renting

The classified ads section of your local paper will probably contain adverts placed by private landlords who wish to rent direct to tenants without going through an agent. These landlords may also put cards in windows of local shops or advertise through your university's accommodation office. You deal directly with the landlord rather than with the university in the case of a head-leased property, or a letting agent in other cases.

Lodging

This is where you live in the same property as your landlord. This may be cheaper than other forms of renting and you may not have to make a separate contribution to household bills as they may be included in your rent. It is essential that you get on with the person with whom you will be lodging, because if a dispute arises at a later date, you may find yourself on the streets with very few rights!

Social Housing

Social Housing refers to accommodation provided by local authorities or Housing Associations. Unfortunately, it is not usually available to students and there is a chronic shortage in many areas of the country. However, if you will be studying at a local university and fit into one of the groups of people who qualify for social housing, or you have enough 'points' on the allocation system, you may be eligible. Contact the Housing Services Department of your local council for more information.

Contracts

Having decided where you are going to live, and whom you will be renting from, you will then probably need to sign a contract. The main exception to this will be if you are lodging with a resident landlord, when a verbal agreement between you will normally be made. Some private landlords who do not let through an agent may not ask you to sign a contract either. As the law students among you will know, whether a contract is in writing or not, a contract will exist between the two parties. In the case of a dispute at a later date, someone with a verbal agreement will have much more difficulty proving what was agreed than a person with a written contract. If you remember only one piece of advice from this chapter, it should be to get a written contract whenever possible!

There are a number of common contracts used in property letting. These are some of the main ones you are likely to come across.

Licence to Occupy

A 'licence to occupy' is exactly that. It allows you to occupy the property, which may be a whole house, a room in a flat or a room in a hall of residence. The licence may have a 'term', which is a start date and an end date, and should specify the amount of rent you have to pay. The licence is a direct contract between you and the landlord, or their agent, so even if the licence is for a room in a house where there are several rooms, you can only be held liable for your own rent – you will see why this is important later on in this chapter. A licence does not grant you 'exclusive occupation', however, so the landlord has the power to come into the property as and when they see fit, usually to provide some sort of 'service'. In halls, this may be for cleaners to come into the room once a week. In many cases, especially if you are lodging, the landlord may not be required by law to give formal notice if they want you to leave, and they will almost certainly not require a court order. So if you have a licence you have very few rights.

Individual Tenancy

An individual tenancy will be a direct contract between you and the landlord or their agent. No other parties will be mentioned unless you have been asked to provide a guarantor (more on that later). As with the licence, this means you can only be held liable for your own rent, not that of any others who live in the same property. An individual tenancy is likely to be granted if a landlord is letting a large property and people are moving in at different times rather than forming one 'household' from the start.

If you have an individual tenancy, you have exclusive occupation of the part of the property specified on the contract.

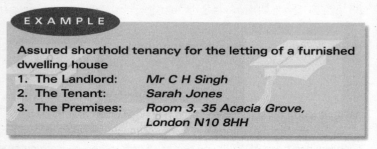

E X A M P L E

Assured shorthold tenancy for the letting of a furnished dwelling house
1. The Landlord: *Mr C H Singh*
2. The Tenant: *Sarah Jones*
3. The Premises: *Room 3, 35 Acacia Grove,*
                       London N10 8HH

The above extract from Sarah Jones's tenancy agreement shows that she has 'exclusive occupation' of Room 3 at 35 Acacia Grove. This means that her landlord must notify her in advance if he needs to gain access to her room to, for example, carry out an inspection or do repairs. Sarah will have use of the common parts of the house, such as the halls and landing, bathroom, kitchen and garden, but will share these with the other tenants. Technically speaking, the landlord can also enter these parts of the property without having to give notice, but it is rare for this to happen.

Joint and Several Tenancies

A 'joint and several' tenancy will have all the tenants' names on one contract.

E X A M P L E

Assured shorthold tenancy for the letting of a furnished dwelling house
1. The Landlord: *Mr C H Singh*
2. The Tenants: *Sarah Jones*
                       Louise Simmonds
                       Michael Parker-Smith
                       Anthony Cooper
3. The Premises: *35 Acacia Grove, London N10 8HH*

As you will see from this example, all four tenants are named on one contract and the property as a whole is listed as 'The Premises' – no reference is made to individual rooms. In this case, Sarah, Louise, Michael and Anthony jointly and severally have exclusive occupation of 35 Acacia Grove. This means the landlord must give them notice before entering the property, unlike the case of the individual tenancy, above, where he only needs to give notice to enter a specific room. However, all four tenants will now also be 'jointly and severally' liable for both the rent and the household bills. If one person moves out and does not find a replacement tenant, the remaining three tenants will have to pay that fourth person's share of the rent, in addition to their own.

These are the most common forms of tenancies and only a brief overview has been given. If you are at all unsure about what you are being asked to sign by a landlord, contact a welfare officer or student adviser, or your local Citizens' Advice Bureau, Independent Advice Centre or Law Centre.

Keeping the Roof Over Your Head

Paying for your accommodation is likely to be the biggest single expense you face as a student, even more than tuition fees. It is important, then, that you understand the sorts of things you have to pay for, why you have to pay them and what could happen if you don't pay. Household bills (and tuition fees) are dealt with in Chapter 10 but what follows here is an outline of charges you are likely to have to pay whilst renting.

Credit Check

If you rent through a letting agent, you may have to pay a fee for a credit check. This can be as high as £30, though it depends on the sort of credit check the agency is going to run. A satisfactory credit check will often be a condition of the agency granting the tenancy and if you either do not pay for the credit check or the result is not to their satisfaction, you will not be allowed to move into the property. A landlord's credit check will often involve:

- Confirming that you have lived where you say you have lived in the past (a Voters Roll Check is usually done) and that the address actually exists. This is to reduce the level of fraud and try to eliminate the risk of the agent taking on 'bad' tenants who are likely to disappear without trace.

● Checking you have no bad and unpaid debts (to assess whether you are likely to pay your rent).

● Giving a recommendation as to whether or not to accept you as a tenant.

If the credit check results are unfavourable, the agent may request a larger deposit.

Deposits

Sometimes known as a bond, surety or security deposit, this is an amount paid at the start of the tenancy which the landlord, or their agent, holds to indemnify themselves against loss or damage arising as a result of the tenant being in occupation. It will usually be a condition of the tenancy that a deposit is paid before you are allowed to move in. The amount charged varies and can be anywhere between, for example, £50 and two months' rent. The maximum that is normally charged is an amount equivalent to one-sixth of the annual rent for the property, or two months. However, a deposit equal to one month's rent is also very common. In some cases, especially if an unsatisfactory credit check result has been received, or if you are an overseas student, a landlord may require a much larger deposit – sometimes the equivalent of six months' rent. Unfortunately, this is not unlawful.

When paying the deposit, you should always ask exactly what it is for and whether or not it is refundable when you move out. There are a number of ways you can protect yourself to help make sure you get your deposit back at the end of the tenancy:

● Ask the landlord for written confirmation that the deposit is refundable and under what, if any, circumstances deductions will be made.

● Agree an inventory with the landlord when you move in – this is a list of the furnishings, fixtures and fittings in the property and a record of their condition. Take photographs if you think it will help.

● Arrange an appointment with the landlord when you are about to move out for them to come and inspect the property and go through the inventory. Deductions will often be made from deposits for alleged damage to furniture. If you have a clear record of the condition of everything when you moved in, you will protect yourself against this happening.

● Make sure the furniture is in the same place when you leave the property as it was when you moved in, and that the property has been thoroughly cleaned – landlords often make deductions from deposits for cleaning. If the property includes a garden, make sure that is in a good state when you leave too!

If anything does become damaged during your tenancy, notify the landlord in writing straight away – do not wait until you are about to move out as you may lose your deposit.

Holding Deposits

Some landlords and agents will ask for payment of a 'holding deposit' whilst contracts are being drawn up, or if you are part of a group and other members have not yet seen the property or signed the contract. In most cases, they will deduct this from the first instalment of rent you have to pay, but not always, so make sure you ask the landlord.

If the landlord subsequently decides not to go ahead with the tenancy, you should be entitled to claim back any holding deposit paid. If the landlord refuses to refund it, however, your only option is to take action via the Small Claims Procedure in the County Court. If this happens to you, seek advice immediately. If you back out of the tenancy having already paid a holding deposit, the landlord may be entitled to retain it, especially if it means they will lose money by not being able to let the property until later. Again, if this happens to you, seek advice straight away.

Agent Fees

If you rent through a letting agent, you may have to pay an agency fee when the contract is signed. They may call it a 'contract fee' or something else. These fees vary enormously and can be as high as £200 in some areas. Unfortunately, if you do decide to rent through a letting agent, you have no choice but to pay their fees so do check exactly what you will have to pay before signing anything. However, they cannot charge you simply for taking your details and sending you information about available property. They can only make a charge if they find accommodation which you accept and for which you subsequently enter into a tenancy agreement.

Adding up Fees and Charges

So far, we have looked at the fees and charges you may have to pay at the start of a tenancy. As you will have seen, renting through the private sector can potentially be very expensive to start off with.

EXAMPLE

Sarah, Louise, Michael and Anthony rent 35 Acacia Grove from Mr Singh, through a letting agent, Dodgy Properties Ltd. They each pay monthly rent of £325, but before moving in, each of them had to find:

Credit check fee	£30
Deposit	£650
Agency fee	£50 (i.e. £200 between the 4 of them)
Plus first month's rent	£325
Total	£1,055

Contrast this with Omar, who is at the same university but living in halls of residence.

Omar's rent is £75 per week. The university takes payment of its halls fees in three instalments in October, January and March, so the only upfront payment Omar needs to make is his halls deposit of £200, a total of £855 less than each of Sarah, Louise, Michael and Anthony.

This is something you need to bear in mind when leaving home for the first time and going to university. Remember that your student loan will not be paid until after you have enrolled on the course but that initial charges to a letting agent will need to have been paid before you move in, which is likely to be before you enrol.

Rent

Last but by no means least! This is quite simple – if you do not pay your rent you may end up without a roof over your head. In many cases, the landlord would need to go through quite an involved process to actually remove you from the property but make no mistake – people do get evicted for not paying their rent. For more about dealing with rent arrears, see Chapter 13.

Your tenancy agreement will tell you how often you have to pay rent. In the private sector, monthly payment tends to be the most common but it might also be four-weekly, fortnightly, weekly or termly. Most universities ask students to pay halls fees in termly instalments in line with student loan payments, under current rules. Students who receive NHS bursaries may be asked to pay monthly, as the bursary is paid monthly.

Some landlords, and many universities, ask for payment by either standing order or direct debit (refer to Chapter 8 if you are not sure what these mean) to make sure the rent is paid on the date it is due. It is, therefore, your responsibility to make sure there is enough money in your bank account on the day *before* the payment is due to be made. This is because standing orders and direct debits are paid out first thing in the morning. If the money is not there to cover the payment, the bank will usually apply an administration charge which can be as much as £35 (per payment that is 'bounced'!), and your landlord may impose interest or penalty charges too. If the landlord is likely to impose these charges, it will be stated in your tenancy agreement.

Other landlords may accept cheque or cash payments. If you do have to pay cash, it is advisable to ask the landlord to record the transactions in a rent book so you have a signed record of what has been paid if there is a dispute later.

SEE ALSO
Chapter 13 – dealing with debt

┌ Parents Pay Attention! – Guarantors ─────────

Some landlords or agents require guarantors before allowing students to enter into a tenancy agreement. They usually want someone with an income above £15,000 so 'it could be you!' If your son or daughter fails to pay their rent, the landlord may come to you for payment. If you do not pay, you could find that both you and your son or daughter are held jointly and severally liable for the debt.

Other Problems

Someone Moving Out If you have an individual tenancy – one with just your name on it – this is not a problem. However, if you have a joint tenancy, where all occupants of the property are named on one contract, then you may have problems if a replacement tenant is not found quickly or the person who has left stops paying their share of the rent. When you sign a joint tenancy, you are agreeing that each of you is jointly liable for the whole rent for the property. So in the case of Sarah, Louise, Michael and Anthony, above, they have a joint tenancy for 35 Acacia Grove. They each pay £325 per month, but the rent for the whole property is £1,300. If, for example, Anthony moved out, the £1,300 would need to be paid by the remaining tenants until a replacement could be found. In this case, they could sue Anthony at the end of the tenancy for the additional cost they have incurred, but if he is still a student they may not actually receive payment. Alternatively, if they had to provide guarantors when taking up the tenancy, the landlord may approach Anthony's guarantors for payment of his share.

'My landlord wants to put the rent up' There are specific rules governing when a landlord can increase the rent. If your tenancy specifies a fixed term – a start date and an end date – the landlord cannot increase the rent during that period without your agreement. Most students have fixed-term tenancy agreements with their landlords.

If you are still in the property after the fixed term has ended on what is called a 'periodic tenancy', the landlord may be able to increase the rent in some circumstances but must give notice before so doing. Seek advice if you find yourself in this situation.

'My landlord won't do any repairs' If there are repairs that need doing, in some cases the landlord has a legal obligation to get them done. If you have a tenancy, as opposed to a licence, it is likely to be covered by section 11 of the Landlord and Tenant

Act 1985. This says that a landlord has a duty to keep in good repair, amongst other things:

- exterior of the property, including doors and windows
- drains and sanitation
- supply of water and heating

If any of these go wrong, the landlord has a duty to put them right, and if he does not he can be fined by the local council. If you are worried about any of these things, contact the Private Sector Tenancy Relations Officer at your local council.

'He still won't do them – can I withhold my rent?'
Probably not. If you withhold rent and arrears accrue, the landlord could issue notice and court proceedings, and eventually get you evicted from the property. You could 'counterclaim' for the inconvenience of the breach of the repairing obligation but you may not win. If the landlord does refuse to carry out repairs, seek advice to see if he is legally obliged to do them. If he is, you should follow this procedure:

- Write to the landlord, giving him a reasonable time (14 days is usually enough) in which to undertake the repair. Send the letter by recorded delivery and keep a copy and a note of the recorded delivery number.
- Use the local telephone directory or Yellow Pages and get written quotes from three local tradesmen.
- Write to the landlord again, enclosing the three quotations, again requesting he gets the work done within a reasonable time (seven days may be enough here). Also state that if he does not do anything, you will get the work done yourself. Once again, send the letter by recorded delivery and keep a copy of the letter and recorded delivery number.
- If the landlord still does not do the repair, go ahead with the lowest-priced quote that you obtained. Make sure you get a receipt for payment from the tradesman.
- Write to the landlord again, enclosing a copy of the receipt, requesting payment by return. Threaten to deduct the amount from the next rent payment if payment is not received by a

certain date. Once again, send it by recorded delivery and keep a copy of the letter and recorded delivery number.

- If the landlord does not pay up, deduct that amount from the next instalment of rent.

By following this method, you will have a clear record of the actions you have taken to get the landlord to undertake the repair. If he later decides to issue proceedings against you for non-payment of rent or for rent arrears, you will be able to demonstrate to the court the reason why the rent was not paid. There are other potential remedies that may be available but they are beyond the scope of this book. Contact the welfare officer or student adviser at your students' union or university for more information.

Top Tips – Keeping a Roof Over Your Head

- Find out exactly what you are paying for before signing anything
- Get a written contract if at all possible
- Pay your rent on time!
- Take an inventory of the property when you move in and get it agreed by the landlord
- Report any defects or items of disrepair straight away
- At the end of the tenancy, get the inventory checked by the landlord so you can get your deposit back

Seek advice if:

- The landlord harasses you
- The landlord refuses to do any repairs
- Someone moves out when you have a joint tenancy
- The landlord tries to increase the rent
- The landlord refuses to give back your deposit at the end of the tenancy

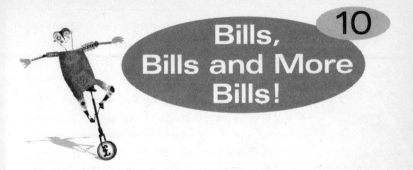

Other than payment of rent, which is likely to be your greatest expense, paying for household bills will probably eat up a sizeable chunk of your income. Even if you are going to be living in halls of residence, you may still have to pay some bills on top of the rent – commonly telephone and possessions insurance, but in some cases you may also have to pay for electricity. In this chapter we look at ways of dealing with household bills so that they do not get out of control, and ways to spread the cost so you do not end up with huge amounts to pay every few months.

Gas and Electricity

Gas and electricity may be included in your rent, especially if the land-lord will be living in the same property as you, or if you are in halls of residence. However, you should check what your tenancy agreement says – in some cases, students in halls need to pay for electricity, and in other cases students renting in the private sector do not have to pay for gas and/or electricity as all bills are included. If you are renting in the private sector and your tenancy agreement does not mention liability for gas and/or electricity, then the bad news is that you will have to pay for it.

Finding Out Who Supplies the Gas and/or Electricity

When you move into a property, you first need to find out who the supplier of gas and/or electricity is. Since the industry was privatised and the market opened up to competition, the supplier could be any one of a number of companies, and some companies who previously supplied only electricity now also supply gas and vice versa. So how do you find out who supplies the gas and/or electricity? Here are some pointers:

- Ask the landlord – they may know and have copies of previous bills
- If you rent through an agent, the agent may know
- If you are in contact with the previous tenants, ask them
- Contact suppliers by telephone to ask if they supply gas and/or electricity to that property

Request a Supply and Open an Account

In many cases, this is as simple as telephoning the relevant company, giving them your name and address, telling them that you have moved in and that you would like a supply of gas and/or electricity. The company then opens the account for you and you can start using the supply immediately. In other cases, the company may request forms of identification from you when setting up the account. If they require this, they will tell you when you contact them. If you have had problems paying for gas or electricity in the past or if there are defaults registered on your credit file (more information in Chapter 13), the company may ask you to pay a deposit before allowing you to have a supply.

In all cases, it is essential that you supply an accurate meter reading when you move in. This is to prevent you from being charged for electricity and/or gas before you moved in and requested the supply. By law, each property must contain a meter if it is supplied with gas and/or electricity. If you receive both gas and electricity then you will have two meters – remember that the same company may not be responsible for the supply of both gas and electricity! There are a number of different sorts of meter used by gas and electricity companies so it is not possible to go into too much detail here. If the meter shows numbers, then that is likely to be the meter reading you need to give. Some modern meters contain a digital LCD display that can tell you a number of things. If this is the case, your supplier will tell you which screen provides the correct meter reading. Older meters have dials, some of which turn anti-clockwise and some clockwise, just to confuse things! There should be arrows on the meter pointing out which dials go in which direction, along with instructions on how to read the meter. Make sure you give the supplier an accurate meter reading as this determines the point from which you will be charged by them. There is nothing worse than an inaccurate meter reading causing an inflated bill a few months later when things are very difficult to prove.

Whose Name Should Go on the Bill?

This is often the biggest bone of contention in shared student houses. The person who is named on the bill is the person with whom the supply company has a contract and is therefore the person most likely to have action brought against them in the case of a dispute. However, it is not that simple as all members of a household can be held liable for payment under a legal doctrine known as 'beneficial user'. This will obviously only happen if any part of the bill remains unpaid. The easiest way to avoid this problem is if all names appear on the bill. Not all companies' computer systems can cope with this, but if there are three or four of you sharing a house, it may be possible – you should check with your gas or electricity company to see how many names they can hold on their system.

Paying the Bill

There are a number of ways that you can pay for gas or electricity. It is best to decide on how you will pay for it when you first move into a property so that the relevant supply company can set up the details on their billing system. The last thing you want is a bill for an entire year's supply of gas or electricity arriving at the end of the summer term when you may not have any money left . . .

Quarterly Bill

The quarterly bill is one of the most common forms of payment for gas and electricity. The gas or electricity company may send somebody to read the meter and bill you accordingly. Alternatively, they might estimate the amount of gas or electricity you have used and send a bill based on that level of consumption. If you have used a substantially different amount, you can contact them with a meter reading and they will adjust the bill accordingly. The bill will have a tear-off slip at the bottom which you send with the payment so that the company knows which account to credit the payment to. You can pay the quarterly bill in a number of ways:

- By sending a cheque and the payment slip to the company in the envelope they provide
- By cash or cheque at the Post Office
- Over the telephone, using a credit or debit card
- By cash or cheque over the counter at a bank (if you do not use your own bank you may have to pay an additional fee to the bank for handling the payment)

Monthly Budget Plan

If you set up a monthly budget plan, you pay a set amount to the supply company each month, usually by direct debit. The company will send you a quarterly statement for information showing the amount of gas or electricity used and the amount paid. If there is a shortfall in payment compared to the actual amount of fuel used at the end of the year, you will need to make up the difference with a one-off additional payment. If there is a credit balance and you are not going to be staying in that property for another year, you may get a refund from the supply company. This payment method often qualifies for discounts.

PayPoint

PayPoint is a payment system that works with a special card supplied by your gas or electricity company. When you receive the bill, you take the bill, the card and your payment in cash to your nearest PayPoint outlet. The retailer will swipe the card through their terminal and ask how much you are paying. You hand over the cash and are given a receipt showing the amount paid. There are now PayPoint outlets in many shops across the country – most commonly in local shops or newsagents. They can be identified by the purple and yellow 'PayPoint' signs either outside the shop or in the window.

PayPoint can be a useful method of payment if you have a large bill which you cannot afford to pay in one go. You need to ask the electricity or gas company if you can pay by this method and they may not agree. However, if you are in a group and you do not have access to direct debit facilities, this can be a useful option for you to consider.

Budget Meter

Budget meters are often controlled with either cards or keys. You take the card or key to the local PayPoint outlet or, in some cases, Post Office, and give the assistant the card or key and payment in cash. They 'charge' the card or key and give you a receipt. When you get home, you insert the card or key into your meter and the payment registers. If you already have a budget meter installed, this will be the only method of payment open to you, but even if you do not have a meter it could be worth considering. If you like, it is almost a 'pay as you go' method but it does have a number of pitfalls:

- If you forget to add credit to your meter and the local PayPoint outlet is closed you will, in effect, disconnect yourself
- It can work out more expensive to pay for gas and electricity through one of these meters
- It can cost up to £150 to have a budget meter installed if there is not one already in the property

For further information on dealing with priority debts like gas or electricity, see Chapter 13.

When You Move Out

On the day you move out, take a final meter reading and notify the gas or electricity company of the reading. They will need a forwarding address so that they can issue a final bill. Remember, many landlords will not return deposits until they have proof that all final bills have been settled, so you may need to show proof of payment to your landlord to get your deposit back.

Water

Payment of water charges may be included in your tenancy agreement so check it carefully. If the agreement specifically mentions that water charges are included in the rent, then the landlord will be liable to pay them, and if a bill is received it should be passed on to the landlord without delay. If the agreement does not say anything about water charges, then you are liable for payment.

Opening an Account

In most cases, you need only contact one company to request a supply. However, in other areas, mains water is the responsibility of one company whilst charges for waste water are paid to another company. Your water company will tell you if this applies. As with gas and electricity, a telephone call may be all that is required, but some companies may require proof of identification or payment of a deposit if you have a bad payment record from the past. Liability for water charges is slightly different from gas and electricity as water companies can make 'The Occupier' of a property liable. To avoid any doubt, you should get the account put into your name as early as possible. Most companies can have several names included on accounts.

How Water is Charged for

Water is charged for in one of two ways – rateable value or metered.

Rateable Value

This refers to the old rateable value of the property (pre-1989) so the higher the rates for the property then, the higher the charge for water now. This will only apply to properties built or converted before 1989.

Metered

Since 1989, all new properties and conversions, such as houses converted into flats, have had to have a water meter installed. Some older properties also have meters fitted if the owners have requested them. If there are more than two people in a property, metered water is likely to be more expensive, though it does of course depend on how much water is actually used.

Paying the Bill

Whether your water charges are based on rateable value or metered amounts, the methods of payment available remain broadly the same.

Annual Bill

The water company issues an annual bill that you pay either in full when it is issued or in two instalments, paid every six months.

Monthly Budget Plan

Paid by direct debit on a monthly basis. Some water companies will also issue payment books that allow charges to be paid at the Post Office or over the counter at a bank. Remember, if you use a bank other than your own, you may have to pay a handling fee.

PayPoint

As for gas and electricity.

Online

Some water companies now let you access your bill information and pay it online.

What if You Don't Pay the Bill?

Unlike gas and electricity, water companies are not allowed to disconnect water supplies for non-payment. They will issue red reminders and 'Final Notices'. If by this stage water charges have still not been paid, then accounts may be referred to solicitors or debt-collection agencies, and County Court proceedings may be issued. If a judgement is obtained against you, you will have difficulty getting access to credit for the next six years.

When You Move Out

Contact the water company or companies and inform them of the date on which you are moving out. They will need a forwarding address for any final bill that is due, or to send a refund if applicable. As with gas and electricity, the landlord may require proof that the final bill has been settled before releasing any deposit.

Land Line Telephone

As with gas and electricity, there are a number of telephone companies. Telephone bills in shared houses can lead to some of the most bitter arguments, especially if there are expensive phone calls that no-one will own up to having made. If you are going to have a shared phone line, it is sensible to come up with some ground rules from the start. One such rule could be keeping a log book by the telephone and making sure everyone records all phone calls they make (and puts their name next to the number so when the bill comes in you know who made the call!).

Setting Up an Account

Most telephone companies will allow only one name on the account. They will also usually ask for a contract to be signed, and if you have had credit problems in the past they may ask for a deposit to be paid or restrict the type of service you can have. Service restrictions commonly include incoming calls only or incoming and free or local calls, to try to prevent you from running up large bills you will have difficulty paying. It is advisable to ask for fully itemised billing so you can work out who is responsible for which calls when the bill does come in.

Paying the Bill

Telephone companies issue bills either every quarter or every month, depending on the company and the type of service you have requested from them. The most common method of payment is to send a cheque to the company (or cheques from each person in the house if you are all paying a share of the bill) or to pay it at the Post Office or bank.

Monthly Budget Account

This works in a similar way to electricity bills in that you pay a fixed amount by monthly direct debit. The telephone company will issue a quarterly statement showing charges incurred and payments made. Companies may also include incentives, such as discounts, for payment by this method.

PayPoint

As for gas and electricity.

What if You Don't Pay the Bill?

Most companies will issue reminders then final notices before referring the account to solicitors or debt collectors for legal proceedings. You may also have your telephone line restricted to incoming calls or disconnected completely. If your line is disconnected and you want it reconnected at a later date, you will have to pay a high connection charge and possibly an additional deposit.

When You Move Out

Notify the telephone company so they can issue a final bill.

Television Licence

Contrary to popular belief, you are not covered by your parents' TV licence whilst you are at university. Therefore, if you are going to be using a television or video recorder you will probably need a TV licence.

Quick Guide – Do You Need a Television Licence?	
Living in halls of residence	If you have a television, you need a licence
Individual tenancy or lodging with a resident landlord	If you have a television in your room, you need a licence. Any TV in a communal area such as a lounge will be covered provided at least one person in the house has their own licence
Joint and several tenancy in a shared house	One TV licence will cover all TVs in the property

As you can see, the rules are quite complicated. You also need to know that even if you have a black-and-white television but also have a video recorder, you must buy a colour TV licence.

How Do I Get a TV Licence?

You can buy a TV licence at your local Post Office or by calling TV Licensing on Freephone 0800 328 2020. Information can be found on their website at www.tv-l.co.uk

Whose Name Should Be on the Licence?

If you are living in halls of residence, have an individual tenancy or are lodging, then the licence should be in your name. If you have a joint tenancy and live in a shared house with a group of other students, the licence can be put in the name of anyone who lives there. However, if that person moves out, the TV licence goes with them as the licence relates to the person, not the address. In this situation, some-one else in the house would need to buy another licence.

Paying for the TV Licence

Post Office

When you buy the licence at the Post Office, you pay the fee in one lump sum. Since April 2003, the cost for an annual colour licence has been £116. The Licence fee is increased every April.

When Buying from TV Licensing

There are a number of payment options when you buy your licence direct from TV Licensing:

- Lump-sum payment, as at the Post Office.
- Quarterly Direct Debit – the cost of the licence is paid in four equal instalments. However, at present this is slightly more expensive as they add a small administration fee to each payment.
- Monthly Budget Plan – paid by monthly direct debit. If you do not have a licence when you join this scheme, you pay for the current licence in five or six monthly instalments, depending on the time of the month you first apply. At present, this would mean payments of about £19.30 per month. After this, you start paying towards the next licence at the rate of about £9.65 per month, and payments continue on a monthly basis until you cancel the scheme.

What if You Don't Buy a Licence?

If you do not receive a visit from a Licensing Inspector, nothing happens. However, inspectors do visit halls of residence regularly and maintain a fairly high profile in areas with large student populations, as in the past many students did not pay the TV licence. If an Inspector does call and finds that you have not got a TV licence, they will leave a notice requiring you to get one within a short specified period. If you do not get a TV licence in that time, they will issue proceedings in the magistrates' court. Bear in mind that these are criminal proceedings! The maximum penalty for not having a TV licence is a hefty fine of up to £1,000. That is more than half a term's student loan payment.

When You Move Out

If you will not need the TV licence for your new house, the current licence still has some time to run and payments are up to date, you may be able to apply to TV Licensing for a refund. If you are moving to a new address, make sure you tell TV licensing.

Council Tax

Like it or not, everybody is liable for Council Tax once they reach the age of 18. However, as with everything, there is a long list of exceptions!

WARNING!

The rules on Council Tax are very complicated and to explain all of them would require a book on its own. For more information, contact a student adviser or the students' union at your university.

Do I Have to Pay it?

Whether you actually have to pay Council Tax depends on a number of factors. If your tenancy agreement specifically states that Council Tax is included, you do not need to do anything, and if a bill arrives you should send it to your landlord without delay.

Students Living in Halls of Residence. Halls are automatically exempt so students living in halls do not have to pay Council Tax. You do not need to do anything as this exemption is automatic.

Full-time Students Living in Shared Houses Where All Occupants are Full-time Students. These students do not have to pay anything either. However, this exemption is not automatic. You need to apply to your University Academic Registry or Student Records Office for a 'Council Tax Exemption Certificate'. This is a special certificate the university produces stating that you are a full-time student and the date your course began and is due to finish. You then need to take this to the Council Tax department at your local council. You should need to do this only once provided you live within the same local council area throughout your study. Remember, if you move to a different council area, you will need to get a new Exemption Certificate for that council.

Full-time Students Living in Shared Houses Where Not All Occupants are Full-time Students. The answer here depends on how many people in the house are not full-time students. If just one person is not a full-time student, the students in the house should still get Exemption Certificates and send them to the local council. There will then be a 25% Single Person Discount applied to the bill.

If more than one person is not a full-time student, then the full Council Tax bill becomes payable. Any full-time students would still be advised to send Exemption Certificates to the local council to show their status, just in case there is a dispute over payment later. Remember, if you start the year as all full-time students and one ceases to be a full-time student during the year, whether it be because they change to part-time study, leave the course or another reason, Council Tax will become payable from the date the person is no longer a full-time student.

Houses in Multiple Occupation. This is a legal term referring to houses where rooms are let on an individual basis. There is no strict definition of what actually constitutes an HMO, and different local authorities interpret the law in different ways. However, if your tenancy is purely for your own room and you have a lock on the door, it is likely the house will be regarded as an HMO. In this case, the landlord will probably have retained liability for the Council Tax but will probably have passed on the additional cost by way of an increase in the rent. Once again, if all the residents in an HMO are full-time students, the landlord will want copies of the Council Tax Exemption Certificate from each person to pass on to the Council.

Living with a Resident Landlord. Whether or not the landlord pays a mortgage or rent, they are higher on the hierarchy of liability set out in the rules governing Council Tax. In this case, you will not be liable for Council Tax but the landlord may well have increased the rent as a result.

Setting up the Account

When you move into the property, you should contact the Council Tax department at the local council and give them the full address of the property, the names of everybody living there and the date you moved in. You should also send in your Council Tax Exemption Certificates as soon as possible to make sure that the correct bill is issued, even if it is a bill for nil.

Paying the Bill

Unless there is a change in liability, Council Tax bills are issued annually, usually between mid-February and mid-March. Payment becomes due at the start of the financial year, 6 April, or the Monday following if 6 April falls at the weekend. Most students move into their accommodation in September so you may receive a Council Tax bill for part of the year. For information on dealing with Council Tax debts, see Chapter 13.

Lump Sum Payments

You can settle the bill, in full, when it is issued.

Monthly Payments

Council Tax can be paid in 10 instalments (April to January, or May to February) if the bill is for the full year. The number of instalments you can pay if the bill is issued at other points in the year will depend on when it is issued. For example, if a bill is issued in September, you will have five months, October through to February, in which to settle it before the new bill is issued for the following year. Methods of payment used include:

- Monthly direct debit
- Monthly payments over the counter at the council's offices
- Monthly payments at the Post Office or a bank
- PayPoint

If you do have to pay Council Tax, check with your council which payment methods they operate as not all councils accept payments by all the above methods.

When You Move Out

Tell the council the date on which you will be moving out. They will probably ask for forwarding addresses for all the tenants. They will then either issue a final bill for the property or a refund if you have paid in advance.

Mobile Phones, Internet, Cable or Satellite TV and Other 'Luxuries'

Do you really need one? Would you regard it as an essential item? If you take out a contract, can you really afford the monthly payments? Do you realise how much they actually cost? These are questions you really need to ask yourself before taking out a contract for a mobile phone that requires you to make monthly payments. It is not uncommon for students who use their mobile phones heavily to run up bills in excess of £100 per month. That is £1,200 per year – more than the current full cost of tuition fees, if you have to pay them. Also, remember that the minimum cost for a basic cable TV package can be as high as £20 per month. For a student on a tight budget, these are all considerations you should take into account before entering into year-long binding contract agreements. If you must have a mobile phone, consider instead a pay-as-you-go type phone, available on all the networks and now roughly the same cost as contract phones.

Paying the Bill

In almost all cases with contract mobile phones, internet service providers and cable/satellite TV, direct debit each month is the only realistic option. Many companies add extra charges if you elect to pay by other methods.

What if I Don't Pay the Bill?

In almost all these cases, the company concerned will disconnect your service and eventually issue legal proceedings through the County Court.

Possessions Insurance

Can you really afford not to have it? Many companies offer special deals for students, whether living in halls of residence or in the private rented sector. In addition, if you have a bicycle, computer or musical instrument, they can offer special extra levels of cover for these items.

The following table shows the cost of an insurance policy as opposed to the cost of replacing items a typical student may have.

Can you afford not to have possessions or contents insurance?			
Cost of replacement if insured		Cost of replacement if not insured	
Insurance policy	£120.00	Computer	£800.00
Excess payment	£100.00	Stereo	£200.00
		50 CDs at £14.99 each	£749.50
		Television	£120.00
		Video recorder	£100.00
		DVD player	£200.00
		10 DVDs at £16.99 each	£169.90
TOTAL COST £220.00		**TOTAL COST £2,339.40**	

As you can see, if you had to buy replacements rather than pay for an insurance policy, you would be paying more than a term's worth of student loan. So, can you *really* afford not to have possessions insurance?

Tuition Fees and Other Course Costs

First, you should establish whether you actually have to pay tuition fees. The information in Chapters 2 to 5 will help you work this out and should also enable you to work out if the level of fees you have been charged is correct.

If You Do Have to Pay Tuition Fees

Find out from your university what their payment terms are – these vary considerably among universities. For 'home' (UK) students, there is usually an instalment plan, commonly of two or three instalments, though some universities will allow fees to be paid in 10 instalments. If your fees are below £250–£300, you may have to pay them in one instalment. Many universities will also insist on payment by direct debit so, as with the student loan, if you are going to be paying your own fees, make sure you open a bank account before going to university. That said, many universities are more flexible over the payment terms they will accept, so check with your university's finance department.

Payment terms for overseas students also vary considerably with some universities requiring payment of a proportion of the fees upfront before enrolment on the course.

Other Fees

Remember, you may have to pay other fees during the course. These can include:

● Library fines – non-payment of these will mean access to library facilities will be blocked so you will not be able to study for your course. If they are outstanding at the end of the academic year, they may be added to any tuition fee debt and therefore subject to the sanctions outlined above.

- Printing and photocopying – you will usually have to pay for these upfront.
- Studio fees – especially common for students on art or music courses. Non-payment could potentially mean the debt is added to any outstanding tuition-fee debt, as above.
- Field trips – you will usually have to pay for these upfront.
- Books and equipment – some students will need to buy specialist books and equipment which may be supplied by the university. If you do not pay for these, the debt could be added to any tuition-fee debt, as above.

Top Tips – Bills

- Do not ignore them – they will not go away
- Pay in instalments by direct debit if possible to make sure the payment is on time and not forgotten about
- Set up a 'house bank account' so that everyone pays an amount into it every month and all the regular bills come out of it
- Make sure you give correct meter readings to gas and electricity companies when moving in and out of a property
- Make sure you send Council Tax Exemption Certificates to the council as soon as possible after moving in
- Pay your tuition fees on time to prevent your university taking further action

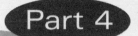

Juggling Your (Limited) Finances

11

The Chancellor of Your Own Exchequer?

(or How to Draw Up a Budget)

Every year, the Chancellor of the Exchequer leaves number 11 Downing Street with his little red box, containing a speech to the House of Commons on how he intends to spend the Government's money in the coming year and how he intends to raise additional income, perhaps from taxation or by borrowing. It may sound a bit grand but the principles are the same for you – it is all about 'balancing the books' or making sure you have enough money to cover your necessary expenses, and identifying when and where savings can be made or additional income gained.

So How Do You Start?

There is a blank Budget Planner in Appendix C for you to copy and use as many times as you like.

For a student in higher education, budgeting is particularly important as you are likely to have uneven income flows. For example, the student loan is currently paid in three roughly equal instalments, though the third term's payment is slightly higher. However, your terms may not be of equal length, especially if your university has an entire semester before Christmas, as some do. This can mean the loan has to last longer in some terms than in others, and as a result you may find you have less to live on per week at some points of the year than at others. Students on NHS-funded courses will face different problems as NHS bursaries are paid monthly over the course of the academic year. So just where do you start?

First, you must decide whether you are budgeting on a weekly, fortnightly, monthly or termly basis. This is vital as all your figures must be for the same period. If you use a mixture of monthly and weekly figures you will end up with an unrealistic budget plan that you will not be able to stick to. In the worst-case scenario, you might even run out of money halfway through the term. Remember, though, that not all income may cover the same period – for example, a student loan will be paid over a term but if you are also working, your wages may be paid weekly, fortnightly, monthly or every four weeks.

EXAMPLE

Ben receives a student loan of £4,930 this year. He receives two instalments of £1,626.90 and a third instalment of £1,676.20.
Term 1 is from 22 September to 12 December (12 weeks plus 3 vacation weeks, 15 in total)
Term 2 is from 5 January to 19 March (11 weeks plus 2 vacation weeks, 13 in total)
Term 3 is from 5 April to 14 May (6 weeks)
In term 1, Ben therefore has £108.46 per week on which to live, in term 2, £125.14 per week and in term 3, £279.36 per week.

EXAMPLE

Esther is studying for a Diploma in Midwifery and receives a bursary from the NHS of £5,432 per year. This is paid to her monthly in instalments of £493.81 (excluding the first instalment).
Esther therefore has £493.81 per month on which to live, or £113.95 per week.

EXAMPLE

Farah is on a degree-level Adult Nursing course and lives with her parents. She receives a means-tested NHS bursary of £1,899 per year, paid monthly in instalments of £172.63 (excluding the first instalment). In addition, she receives a reduced-rate student loan of £1,465 paid in three instalments, 2 x £483.45 and 1 x £498.10.

Her term dates are the same as Ben's (above) for the first two terms (15 weeks and 13 weeks respectively). Her third term is from 5 April to 16 July (15 weeks).

As Farah's income is from two different sources, she needs to work out what her total income for each term will be. Assuming her bursary is paid on the 10th of each month, in term 1 she receives a loan of £483.45 plus 3 payments of the bursary of £172.63. Her total income is therefore £1,001.34, giving a weekly income of £66.75.

She has the same income in term 2, but there are only 13 weeks, so her weekly income is £77.02 per week. In term 3, she receives 4 bursary payments and a student loan payment of £498.10. There are 15 weeks, so her weekly income in term 3 is £79.24.

So, as you can see, income can vary over the course of the year. It makes sense to work out a budget for each term so you can identify early on in the year where there may be problems. Make sure you add together all your income sources, including:

- Student loans
- Contributions from parents, partner or family
- NHS bursaries
- Social work bursaries
- Opportunity Bursaries or HE Grants, Assembly Learning Grants, HE bursaries or Young Students' Bursaries
- Income from part-time work
- Scholarships and trust funding
- Supplementary allowances such as Adult Dependants' Grants or childcare grants
- Any state benefits
- Tax credits
- Income from savings and investments

Top Tips – Converting Amounts

From ▶ To ▼	Weekly	Fortnightly	Four-weekly	Monthly	Termly	Yearly
Weekly		Divide by 2	Divide by 4	Multiply by 12 then divide by 52	Divide by number of weeks in term	Divide by 52
Fortnightly	Multiply by 2		Divide by 2	Multiply by 12 then divide by 26	Divide by number of weeks in term then multiply by 2	Divide by 26
Four-weekly	Multiply by 4	Multiply by 2		Multiply by 12 then divide by 13	Divide by number of weeks in term then multiply by 4	Divide by 13
Monthly	Multiply by 52 then divide by 12	Multiply by 26 then divide by 12	Multiply by 13 then divide by 12		Divide by number of weeks in term then multiply by 52 and divide by 12	Divide by 12
Termly	Multiply by number of weeks in term	Divide by 2 then multiply by number of weeks in term	Divide by 4 then multiply by number of weeks in term	Multiply by 12 then divide by 52 and multiply by number of weeks in term		Divide by 52 then multiply by number of weeks in term
Yearly	Multiply by 52	Multiply by 26	Multiply by 13	Multiply by 12	Divide by number of weeks in term then multiply by 52	

Of course, this list is not exhaustive and you may well have other sources of income that you are using to support yourself whilst studying. Include those in any budget plan you draw up to get a whole picture. Once you have done this, you will have a good idea of what money you have available.

> **EXAMPLE**
>
> Damian is working out his income for the first term of the academic year.
> He knows he receives the following:
>
> > Student loan: £990 this term
> > Parental contribution: £450 this term
> > Scholarship: £500 this term
> > Income from part-time work: £70 per week
>
> Damian wants to work out his weekly budget. His term dates are 22 September to 19 December and his next student loan will be received on 12 January. He therefore needs to budget for 16 weeks. The income side of his budget sheet would look like this:
>
> | Income Source | Weekly Amount |
> | --- | --- |
> | Student loan | £61.87 |
> | Parental contribution | £28.12 |
> | Scholarship | £31.25 |
> | Part-time work | £70.00 |
> | Total weekly income | £191.24 |
>
> Damian knows, therefore, that he has £191.24 per week to live on this term.

Expenditure

Now that you have worked out the money you have coming in, you need to calculate how much you have going out. Make sure you use the same period for your outgoings as you did for your income, otherwise you will find either a large surplus – and temptation for a bout of serious retail therapy – or a large shortfall between your income and expenditure, and panic setting in. Remember also that your list of expenditure items is likely to be somewhat longer than your list of sources of income. Don't let this get you down too much – it is very common. Some of the things you are likely to need to include as expenditure items are:

- Rent or other accommodation costs, such as halls fees or mortgage payments
- Gas
- Electricity
- Water
- Council Tax
- Telephone
- Mobile phone
- Contents insurance
- Housekeeping – including food, toiletries and household goods
- Laundry
- Tuition fees, if you are liable to pay them
- Field-trip costs
- Photocopying and printing
- Books and other equipment
- Meals and drinks whilst on campus
- Public transport
- Car costs
- Visits home
- Clothing and footwear
- Sports clubs and hobbies
- Entertainment and socialising
- Childcare
- Children's school meals

Once again, this list is certainly not exhaustive and you should include all items of expenditure to make sure your budget is realistic. If you smoke, you will need to include the cost of cigarettes in your budget or else you will soon find that you cannot keep to your planned budget and start getting into difficulty.

One problem you may find with working out your regular expenditure is that you have different payment periods for certain items. For example, you might pay rent monthly, utility bills every quarter and tuition fees, if you have to pay them, in two or three instalments, depending on payment plans offered by your university. Use the conversion chart shown earlier in this chapter to convert your figures. Remember that a quarter is equivalent to three months.

EXAMPLE

Damian is now working out his expenditure. He spends the following:

Rent:	£250 per month
Gas and electricity:	£8 per week (approximately)
Water:	£5 per month
Mobile phone:	£25 per month
Housekeeping:	£35 per week
TV licence:	£9.62 per month
Laundry:	£2.80 per week
Tuition fees:	£1,125 over the course of the academic year (3 instalments)
Books etc.:	£10 per week (on average)
Drinks and food at college:	£5 per week
Public transport:	£6 per week
Clothes:	£30 per month
Entertainment:	£20 per week

As Damian has worked out his income on a weekly basis, he needs to calculate his expenditure on a weekly basis as follows:

Expenditure Item	Weekly Amount
Rent:	£57.70
Gas and electricity:	£8.00
Water:	£1.15
Mobile phone:	£5.77
Housekeeping:	£35.00
TV licence:	£2.22
Laundry:	£2.80
Tuition fees:	£21.64
Books etc.:	£10.00
Drinks and food at college:	£5.00
Public transport:	£6.00
Clothes:	£6.92
Entertainment:	£20.00
Total weekly expenditure:	£182.20

When you look at Damian's income, you will see he has £191.24 per week. He has budgeted very well for the term, and if he keeps to his budget plan he should not get into any difficulties, unless anything unexpected happens.

If Damian had not managed to budget so well and had ended up with a shortfall between his income and expenditure, he would have needed to take action to prevent himself getting into debt.

Increasing Income

This will be looked at in more detail in Chapter 12 but you could do the following:

- Check to make sure you have the correct amount of student loan – many students do not realise if they have been incorrectly assessed by the LEA/ELB/SAAS and lose out as a result. Your student services department or students' union should be able to help you with this.
- Check to see if you are entitled to any bursaries, grants or scholarships.
- Ask your parents or other family members if they are able to help.
- Ask the bank for an overdraft facility, preferably before going overdrawn so you do not incur charges.
- Get a part-time job during evenings and weekends or increase hours if you already have a job.

Minimising Expenditure

Once you have looked at ways of increasing your income, you could try to find ways of reducing your expenditure. Some things you will not be able to change, such as the amount of rent you pay, as you will probably be tied into a contract for a fixed period. However, if your tenancy does not have a fixed term and you feel you are paying too much for your accommodation, you could always look for somewhere cheaper to live. Remember, though, that you will need to give the correct amount of notice to your landlord and you might have to keep paying rent until another tenant moves in to replace you. If you have dependent children or are disabled, see if you can apply for Housing Benefit to reduce the amount of rent you have to pay. Do not be put off if staff at the council tell you that you are not eligible – ask them for the forms anyway. Many student advisers in universities and students' unions will be able to give you an estimate of your likely Housing Benefit entitlement.

Similarly, you may not be able to reduce the amount, if any, of tuition fees you have to pay to your university. But you can:

- Check that your LEA/ELB/SAAS has assessed your parents', partner's or your own income correctly. If there has been a change in circumstances and the income has now reduced significantly, you may be entitled to have your fee liability reassessed and perhaps reduced or even completely eliminated.
- Ask your parents or other family members if they are able to pay the fees or at least help you with paying them.
- Negotiate a payment plan with your university's Finance Department to try to reduce the amount you have to pay in one go.

Other Expenditure Items

Gas and Electricity It is estimated that the average single person will spend about £6 to £8 per week on gas and electricity together. If you estimate that you are spending more than this, it could be worth looking at ways of saving money, perhaps by:

- Switching off electrical appliances rather than leaving them on standby mode
- Switching off lights when you do not need them
- Boiling only the amount of water you need, rather than a full kettle
- Using 'energy saving' light bulbs – more expensive to buy initially but they last longer than ordinary light bulbs and use less electricity

If you have tried all of the above and still think you are paying far too much, contact the gas or electricity company and ask if they can come and look at the meter to see if it is working properly. It is not unheard of for meters to be faulty and charging more for gas or electricity than they should.

Water It is very unlikely that you will be able to reduce the amount you pay in water charges, especially if your bill is based on the rateable value of the property. However, if you have a meter, there are ways you can lower the bill, mainly by reducing the amount of water that is just thrown away. Look carefully at how you use water and see if you can make any savings. One money-saving tip is to place a household brick in the toilet cistern as this reduces the amount of water used when flushing. Remember, little things add up! If you think the bill may be high because of a leak, contact the water company immediately.

Council Tax If you do have to pay Council Tax, see Chapter 10 for information on how to reduce the amount you have to pay.

Telephone It is a good idea to get premium-rate numbers barred as they can cost up to £2 per minute and can lead to arguments in the house if everyone denies that they made these calls. Ask the telephone company for a fully itemised bill and keep a log of all calls made. Avoid long calls to mobile phones as they are very expensive. If you need to make calls to foreign countries, it can be worthwhile buying international calling cards as these often work out much cheaper than calling direct from an ordinary or a mobile telephone, and you can 'pay as you go' rather than being hit with a hefty bill later on.

Mobile Phones Use them sparingly. Advisers see many students with contract mobile phone bills in excess of £100 per month. Can you *really* afford that? Remember that calls to mobiles on other networks can be very expensive, up to 50p per minute in some cases, and that calls are often more expensive during the day than in the evening. Shop around for the cheapest deals, depending on how you are likely to use the phone. Pre-pay deals are often better than contract phones for students as you do not need to continue making regular payments just for being connected and able to receive incoming calls. You will be able to receive calls even if you cannot make outgoing calls until you have bought more credit – this can be a useful money-saving device and make you think before making that call!

TV Licence Refer to Chapter 10 to see if you need to buy a TV licence. Remember that the easiest way to pay for a TV licence is by monthly direct debit.

Laundry If you have to use a launderette it makes sense to wait until you have enough clothes to fill a machine, rather than doing half-loads or single items. If you do your laundry at home, remember that tumble driers use a lot of electricity, so if you can dry the clothes on a line or on the radiators you will save money. If you have the option, of course, you could always ask Mum to do it all for you!

Housekeeping The average single person spends about £25 to £35 per week on housekeeping, which includes food and drink, toiletries and household goods. If you have children or special dietary requirements, you will spend more than this, depending on the nature of your requirements or the number of children in the family. As a rough estimate, allow about £15 per week extra for each child. It can be quite difficult to work out exactly how much you spend on housekeeping so for a period of, say, four weeks, keep all itemised till receipts from supermarkets, showing exactly what you have bought, where you bought it and how much you have spent. You will be amazed and possibly shocked at how quickly it all adds up!

Top Tips – Housekeeping

- If you live in a shared house, buy in bulk and you will benefit from economies of scale and save money
- 'Economy' or own-label goods are often just as good, and in some cases better, as branded goods – in many cases you are only paying for fancy packaging or the name
- Markets can be the cheapest places to buy fresh fruit and vegetables – and the produce is often fresher than that sold in the supermarket
- Avoid expensive pre-prepared ready meals and cook for yourself – you will save *lots* of money
- Take advantage of 'Buy One Get One Free', '3 for 2' or supermarket loyalty card offers, but only on things you know you will actually use! (it is often a good way of stocking up on toiletries and household goods)
- Towards the end of the day, supermarkets often reduce the price of fresh produce which can save you money – especially as most of it can be put in the freezer when you get home

---

After your four weeks of receipt-keeping, look through them carefully. Is there anything you bought that you have not used and are not likely to use? Was everything necessary at the time? How much of the shopping was done on an empty stomach? This is never a good idea as you will fill the basket or trolley with all sorts of things you don't need simply because you are hungry. If possible, always have at least a light snack before going shopping. If you will be living in shared accommodation or in self-catered halls of residence, it makes sense to learn how to cook before going to university. Being able to cook even basic meals can save you quite a lot of money over the year compared to the cost of expensive ready meals. Your local bookshop will stock plenty of 'student' cookbooks and others that contain excellent money-saving ideas for cooking on a limited budget – these include *The Essential Student Cookbook: 400 Budget Recipes to Leave Home With* by Cas Clarke; *Student Grub* by Jan Arkless; and *The Survival Guide to Cooking in the Student Kitchen* by Susan Crook. It is well worth investing in one of these books before leaving for university or, even better, asking your parents to invest in one for you!

Remember that many local 'convenience stores' may be more expensive places to shop than supermarkets. Some supermarkets are also more expensive than others, so do shop around – you will be surprised at how much the price of a basket of basic goods can vary between supermarkets. 'Discount' supermarkets, often foreign companies, are now in many towns. Whilst you might not be able to buy brand-name goods in these stores, they can be a good place to buy basic items thanks to their low prices.

Meals and Drinks in College If you are going to be on campus for a long period of the day you will obviously need to account for some food and drink. How about taking a packed lunch with you? You will be amazed at how much you can save in just the course of a week!

Books and Equipment There is probably not much you can do to reduce your expenditure on essential books and items of equipment as you will need them to complete your course successfully. However, sometimes it can be possible to buy second-hand key textbooks from other students who have already finished with them. You need to be careful that the course tutors are still recommending the same books and that a new edition has not been printed (as is often the case with law textbooks, for example) before parting with hard cash. However, even if the book is the previous edition, it can still be useful for background reading at home where your university library has the up-to-date version available for you to borrow. Another useful money-saving idea is to 'book pool', where you get together with a group of friends and share books amongst you. This can be most useful if you live near each other or even in the same house or halls of residence and are doing the same course. Also ask yourself if you really need that particular book – can you get by with using the library copy as and when you need it?

Photocopying and Printing Charges Do you *really* need to photocopy such a large chunk of the key text? Photocopying charges are typically between 6p and 9p per page, depending on your university. Obviously, if you need pages from a reference-only book, such as an academic journal or law report, then you might need to pay for photocopying. Similarly, if you print off your work whilst on campus using university facilities, you may have to pay up to 10p per page. If you have your own computer and printer at home, it might be cheaper to print work there rather than on campus.

Many universities now make their journals and law reports available online, and you may even be able to read them from home if you have internet access there. This can often help significantly reduce the costs involved in printing and copying reference material.

Public Transport Season tickets are often cheaper than individual tickets and can mean that you save quite a bit of money. Check what the savings are with your local operators. In many areas, students qualify for reduced fares.

Entertainment Whether it be going out clubbing, to the pub, cinema, bowling or just 'down the union bar', you need to budget for some form of entertainment. If you do not include it in your budget, you will be fooling yourself. The budget will not be realistic and, more importantly, you will definitely not stick to it! What items you include will obviously depend on what you do. If, for example, you play in a sports team and have to pay match or coaching fees, you will need to include these in your budget. On the other hand, if your social life involves a couple of nights a week in the union bar, include that. However, any amount you include should be realistic and a true reflection of what you actually spend. If it is too high, think of ways to reduce the spending, either by cutting back or by finding cheaper ways of enjoying yourself.

Top Tips – Going Out on a Budget

- Drink before you go out. It will be cheaper!

- Take out the money you will need before you leave

- Leave your cash card at home to stop the temptation of getting more money out after you have had a few!

- Take advantage of student deals at cinemas, clubs etc. You can often save up to 25% on entrance fees and you can get in free to some clubs

---

Once you have addressed your expenditure, work out the weekly total again. Hopefully, you now have a surplus. If you do not, you should contact a student adviser at your university or students' union for further help and assistance.

But What About Debts?

You will notice that so far we have not looked at regular debt payments, such as loans, HP or finance agreements, or credit cards. Hopefully, you will not have any of these to include in a budget plan but if you do, work out what your minimum contractual payments are each month and add them to your regular expenditure. If you can include them with no difficulties then you have no problems. However, for many students, meeting the minimum payments on credit cards and loans can be extremely difficult. Obviously, the best advice is not to take out these forms of credit in the first place as they can work out to be very expensive. If you do have them and find yourself in difficulty, there are steps you can take to reduce the problems. Further information and advice can be found in Chapter 13.

Quick Guide – Budgeting

- Work out your income and expenditure using the same figures (i.e. weekly, monthly etc.)

- Make sure you have all your entitlements in terms of student loan and other student support funding

- See if you are entitled to any discretionary funds (see Chapter 12)

- Reduce expenditure where possible

- If you have problems with any debts, see Chapter 13

- Seek advice if you get stuck or into difficulties

'Please Sir, I Want Some More!'

Raising More Money

By now, you should have a good understanding of what funding is available for courses of higher education, regardless of which part of the UK you come from and what course you will be studying. You may also have realised that the money provided by the Government will not cover all your expenses whilst you are studying and, having cut back your spending to the absolute minimum, you need more money! This chapter will give you some ideas of ways to increase your income.

SEE ALSO
Chapter 6 – funding from statutory and non-statutory sources, in particular the sections on benefits, tax credits and charitable trusts

Part-time Work

Part-time work remains one of the best and easiest ways of supplementing your income whilst studying. The amount you earn obviously depends on a number of factors, including the availability of work in the local area, your course timetable and workload, and local labour-market conditions determining the level of pay in certain jobs. That said, there is usually a plentiful supply of part-time work in towns and cities where there are high numbers of students. In some areas, employers actively target universities and colleges seeking people to take on part-time work.

How Do I Find it?

There are a number of ways you can find part-time work.

Top Tips – Finding Part-time Work

- Asking in local shops, pubs and other businesses
- University departments, especially libraries, often need additional part-time help
- Notice boards at your university
- Local papers
- University Job Shop (many universities have these)
- University Careers Service
- Students' union – who do you think work behind the bar? That's right, students!
- The internet
- Local radio
- Job Centre or Jobcentre Plus
- Personal contacts

If your university has a Job Shop, that can be an excellent place to start looking, and some jobs can pay quite well. You might even find a job relevant to your course and thus gain additional skills that will be really useful once you finish your course. Remember, a graduate with relevant work experience is likely to be snapped up by employers. Part-time work can, therefore, bring benefits other than immediate financial ones.

Examples of Part-time Jobs for Students

- Bar work – either in town or in the students' union on campus
- Shop work – either in town or on campus
- Telesales
- Market research
- Course-related jobs, such as:
  - o Drama students working in a theatre box office
  - o Sports science students working in a leisure centre
  - o Nursing students doing care work

A job that is related to your course will bring financial benefits as well as enhancing your employability once you have finished the course!

How Many Hours?

In most cases, it will depend on what is available and how many hours you can work without your studies suffering. Many universities recommend that students work no more than between 15 and 20 hours per week in addition to studying full-time. If you are studying part-time, you may be able to work full-time if you can fit it in around your hours of study. If your course has only two or three lectures or tutorials per week and does not involve much private study (which is rare!), you may be able to devote more time to paid work. Once again, it will depend on the need of the employer and whether you think you can cope with the work and the study.

Overseas Students

Students from overseas do have a restriction on the number of hours they can work which is imposed by the UK Government. To a large extent, the number of hours you can work depends on the immigration stamp in your passport. As a general guide, if it contains a *prohibition* on work, you are not allowed to work at all. If your passport contains a *restriction* on work, which usually says that work must be authorised by the Secretary of State, you should be able to work up to 20 hours per week during university term time and as many hours as you are able during vacations. As with everything there are exceptions to these rules, so if you are from overseas and wish to work, seek advice from your international students' adviser or students' union. European Union students are not normally subject to these rules and can work as many hours as they like, the same as UK students.

Vacation Work

Working during the vacations can help you to repay any overdraft you have built up during the previous term as well as allowing you to save for the coming term. If you do not have any coursework or exam revision to do you can work more hours during the vacations, availability of work permitting of course.

How Much Can I Expect to Earn?

This depends on a number of factors including the local labour market – some jobs may pay higher in some areas than in others – and the number of hours you work. However, by law you should be earning at least the National Minimum Wage which is the absolute minimum the Government says employees can be paid for the work they do. For further information on the current rate of the National Minimum Wage, ask your students' union or local Job Centre or Jobcentre Plus. There are two different rates, depending on your age, and the minimum for people aged under 21 is lower than for people over 21. Many employers, however, have decided to pay the higher rate to all staff.

How Will I Be Paid?

This depends on the type of work you are doing and the policy of the employer concerned. It is standard practice for employers to make monthly payments in arrears by direct transfer to a bank account, but that is not always the case so ask your employer. Some employers can pay wages weekly, which is obviously a great help with budgeting.

Income Tax and National Insurance

Contrary to popular belief, students are not automatically exempt from paying income tax and national insurance. The rules are very complicated but here is a summary:

- If you earn less than the 'lower earnings limit', you will not pay any national insurance contributions
- If you earn more than the 'lower earnings limit' you will pay national insurance contributions, and unless you are self-employed, these will be deducted from your pay by your employer
- You will be liable to pay income tax if your income is above your 'personal allowance' notified to you by the Inland Revenue

From April 2003 to April 2004, the basic personal allowance for a single person is £4,615. This means that the first £4,615 of earnings are not taxed. Student loans and other student support funding are not included in this figure so it relates solely to money earned from work and any interest from savings and investments. Your employer will usually deduct income tax from your pay automatically. It is therefore very important that when you start work you give them proof of your national insurance number and a P45 if you have one. If you have worked previously, your last employer would have given you a P45 when you were leaving. This is a special Inland Revenue form that tells you and your new employer how much you have earned that tax year, how much income tax and national insurance has been paid and what your 'tax code' is. A tax code is used by the Inland Revenue to tell an employer how much tax to deduct from an employee's wages and keeps your exact details confidential to the Inland Revenue. If you do not have a P45 to give your new employer, they will ask you to fill in a P46, which they send to the Inland Revenue to find out your tax code. If you do not fill in this form or provide a P45, you may have to pay 'emergency' tax at a higher rate and lose money as a result. You therefore need to keep any Inland Revenue documents in a safe place.

If you know that during the tax year your earnings will be below your personal tax allowance, you can ask your employer for a form called a P38(S). This is a declaration that you are a full-time student and that for the duration of that tax year you expect your earnings to remain below the limit for income tax. This then means that your employer will pay your wages without deducting income tax. You will still, however, have to pay national insurance contributions. If you are going to fill in a P38(S), you need to be absolutely certain that your earnings will not go above your personal allowance limit. If they do, you will find that you pay tax on all your income once your allowance is exhausted. It can often be quite a blow to see a large chunk of your hard-earned cash swallowed by the taxman! Alternatively, if you only work a few weeks of the year, such as during the vacation, or if your earnings are only slightly over the personal allowance limit, you may be able to claim a tax refund at the end of the year. To do this, you need a P50, which you can get from your local Inland Revenue Enquiry Centre or tax office. Some student advice centres in universities and students' unions also have stocks of this form.

Your employer will issue a form called a P60, which is a statement of the money you have earned and the income tax and national insurance contributions you have made in the last year. If you think you are entitled to a tax refund, use these details to fill in your P50 and send it to your tax office. Remember that your tax office is not necessarily your local office but the office your employer deals with. For example, for many companies in London, the tax office is in Bradford or Middlesbrough, so check the address listed on your P60. Tax refunds do take a while to process but if you are entitled to one, the Inland Revenue will send you a cheque.

Hall Seniors

Some universities employ students, especially final year or postgraduates, as Hall Seniors, sometimes known as Hall Wardens or Resident Tutors. In return for carrying out a certain number of duties each week, hall seniors receive either a reduction in the amount of rent they have to pay or payment. This can provide a valuable additional source of income, or rent reduction, at a time when you need to concentrate more on your studies. It can also provide valuable work experience that will enhance your CV! Ask your university's accommodation office for more information about becoming a hall senior.

Family

For many students, other members of the family are often able to help out financially. Your parents or partner may have been assessed as having to make a contribution towards either tuition fees or living costs or both, depending on their income. Details of how this contribution is worked out can be found in Chapter 2 (if you are from England or Wales), Chapter 3 (if you are from Scotland) and Chapter 4 (if you are from Northern Ireland). However, sometimes parents or other family members are willing and able to help even further. If other family members do offer to help, consider asking the following:

- If they are offering to pay for tuition fees, ask them to pay it direct to your university so you are not tempted to spend it on something else.

- If they are offering to pay your rent, ask them to pay it direct to your landlord so you are not tempted to spend it on something else.
- If they are offering to help with your living costs, consider asking for a regular payment rather than a lump sum at, for example, the start of each term. If they are able to pay in smaller and more regular amounts, it will be easier for you to budget and actually keep to it, rather than receiving a lump sum, heading to the nearest shopping centre and spending it all in one go.

Selling Assets

This is often a last resort but can be a useful way of raising a lump sum quickly if you need it. The main asset you might have is a car. You have to pay for road tax, MOT, insurance, petrol and repairs. When you add it all up, it can be quite a drain on your limited finances. Ask yourself if you really need it and if the answer is 'no', consider cutting your losses and selling it and cashing in any remaining road tax or insurance. In many university towns and cities there is excellent public transport so a car will probably not be necessary unless you are unable to use public transport because of a disability, or you have children.

Bank Overdrafts

If you have a student bank account, chances are you have access to an interest-free overdraft. Most of the high street banks that offer student bank account facilities will automatically authorise an overdraft when opening the account, but you should check with your bank that this is the case with your account before going overdrawn.

Overdrafts are useful for short-term problems, such as your student loan running out just before the end of term. If you have only a few weeks before the next payment, the overdraft facility can tide you over. However, many students need to use their overdraft facility much more than that to meet shortfalls between income and expenditure.

Top Tips – Bank Overdrafts

- ALWAYS ask your bank before going overdrawn for the first time. Penalty charges for unauthorised overdrafts can be very high.
- Know your overdraft limit and keep within it.
- Do not write cheques or use a debit card if you know you will exceed your limit – you will be charged and transactions may be declined, which can be very embarrassing.
- Ask your bank before exceeding any overdraft limit and show them how you intend to repay it and why you need it – they are more likely to agree to your requests if they can see a genuine reason for extending the overdraft and have evidence that some money will be coming in to repay it soon.
- If you receive letters from the bank saying you have gone overdrawn without permission, do NOT ignore them – look in Chapter 13 for more advice.

Help from Your University

Universities administer additional funds on behalf of the Government that they can use to help students in financial need. These are known as 'Access and Hardship Funds' and, depending on which country of the UK you study in, they may be called:

- Hardship Loans (UK-wide but for 2003/04 only)
- Hardship Funds (England and Scotland)
- Access to Learning Fund (England)
- Financial Contingency Funds (Wales)
- Support Funds (Northern Ireland)
- Mature Students' Bursary Fund (Scotland)
- Learner Support Funds (if you are on a further-education course)

Students on degree-level NHS courses in England may also be able to apply for discretionary NHS Hardship Grants, usually administered by your university. Students in England on certain postgraduate teacher training courses may be entitled to Secondary Shortage Subject Scheme (SSSS) funds.

Hardship Loans and other Access and Hardship Funds

As the names suggest, these funds are available to help students in hardship.

Hardship Loans

A Hardship Loan (to be abolished after the end of the 2003/04 academic year) is a payment of up to £500 that full-time students can apply for if they are in financial difficulty. Each university has its own procedures for deciding whether a student is 'in hardship' so payment of a Hardship Loan is not guaranteed. You must have taken out your full student loan entitlement before applying for a Hardship Loan, and you must complete an application and provide certain evidence to the university. Evidence that is usually required includes:

- LEA financial assessment form
- Payment schedule letter issued by SLC showing when you receive your student loan instalments
- Three months' worth of bank statements for all your accounts

You complete a special form which your university authorises and sends to SLC who make payment into your bank account, usually within seven to ten working days. As it is a loan, the Hardship Loan is added to your total student loan amount and you repay it after you finish your course under the same terms as the main student loan. You can find more information about repayment of student loans in Chapter 15.

Other Access and Hardship Funds

The other Access and Hardship Funds are usually non-repayable grants, but in some cases may be given as short-term loans that are paid back to the university. This is often the case if the first instalment of the student loan is late for any reason. Many universities target their funds to certain groups of students, commonly:

- Final-year undergraduate students
- Students who have high course, travel or accommodation costs
- Students with dependants

- Mature students with financial commitments before starting their courses
- Disabled students (especially where the DSA does not meet the full support needs)
- Students who were in care before going to university

Of course, this list does not cover all circumstances, and your university will be able to give you more information. Even if you are not in one of the target groups, you can still apply for assistance. As with the Hardship Loan, you must have to have taken out your full entitlement of student loan and, in 2003/04, students under 25 will be expected to have taken out a Hardship Loan before applying for further assistance from the Access and Hardship Funds. If you are studying part-time, you must be doing at least 60 credit points or 50% of the full-time equivalent course (25% if you are disabled) to be able to apply for assistance. You must also be a 'Home' student (as outlined in Chapter 1) – students from European Union and overseas countries are not able to apply for help from the Access and Hardship Funds.

Each university uses its own assessment process to see if a student qualifies for assistance from these funds but many base their decisions on an income and expenditure analysis. They will look at what income you have and what items of essential expenditure you have. If there is a shortfall, you may get an award, although that award may not cover the entire shortfall. Remember, there is only a certain level of funding available so universities place a limit on the amount of a shortfall they can cover, and there is no guarantee that you will receive anything at all. Universities require documentary evidence of your circumstances so, as with the Hardship Loan, it is essential that you keep things like bank statements and other important documentation such as tenancy agreements and utility bills. Applications for Access and Hardship Funds are usually dealt with by the student services department of your university but check first where you need to apply.

For students studying in Scotland, there is the additional Mature Students' Bursary Fund that can assist with the costs of formal or registered childcare, housing or 'excess' travel (such as the additional costs of taking children to and from the place of childcare when you are on your course). Maximum payments are around £2,000 but do vary depending upon your circumstances. For more information on the Mature Students' Bursary Fund, contact your university in Scotland.

Secondary Shortage Subject Scheme

This is a special fund available to students from the UK or European Union who are on initial teacher-training courses at secondary level. It is only available if you specialise in a subject where there is currently a shortage of teachers at secondary level. In June 2003, the list included the following subjects:

- Applied ICT
- Applied science
- Design and technology
- Engineering
- Geography
- Information and communications technology
- Manufacturing
- Mathematics
- Modern foreign languages
- Music
- Religious education
- Science

Your course must lead to Qualified Teacher Status (QTS) and is only available to students studying in England. Applications are dealt with by the university or college providing the initial teacher training so contact your university or college for more information. As with Access and Hardship Funds, procedures vary across the country.

13

In the Red . . .

Dealing with Debt

Like it or not, you will probably end up in debt at some stage, whether it is during your time in higher education or at some point afterwards. If you buy a home, you will probably take out a mortgage and therefore have a debt. If you choose to pay a bill or for goods in instalments, such as Council Tax, you will have a debt. If you have taken out a student loan during your period of study, you will have a debt. However, if you are up to date with repayments, you may not consider that you have a debt. Instead you will probably think of the payments you make as part of your essential monthly expenditure. After all, a student loan repayment is deducted from your salary by your employer, and a mortgage or Council Tax payment is likely to be paid by direct debit every month. For most people, these 'debts' do not cause a problem. However, if you miss a payment or find that you do not have the income to meet the monthly payments, and therefore get into difficulty, you may then consider yourself 'in debt'.

For students, it is very tempting and easy to get credit. Many high-street shops offer store cards; some credit card companies offer special student deals; and student bank accounts often come with interest-free overdrafts. It does not take a genius to work out that having to make a couple of store card payments and a credit card payment each month will stretch your limited finances even further, perhaps to the point where you think you cannot cope. This is often one of the first 'symptoms' of a problem. A credit card payment is missed and a reminder letter is sent by the card company. You do nothing. A second monthly payment is missed and a stronger letter is sent by the card company. Again, you do nothing. A third payment is missed and the credit card company issues a Default Notice, demanding immediate repayment of the entire balance. You panic and use the next month's rent payment to pay the credit card. You miss a rent payment as a result and, before long, receive a Notice Seeking Possession from your landlord with the threat of court proceedings for eviction due to unpaid rent. It is easy to see just how desperate things can get if you do not deal with them.

Avoiding Debt in the First Place

The old saying 'prevention is better than cure' is no more relevant than when looking at debt. If you do not give in to temptation and get into debt, you will not have a problem. Many of the main tips on sound budgeting and money management are equally applicable to avoiding debt.

Top Tips – Avoiding Debt

- Do not get a credit or store card
- Do not take out expensive loan agreements to buy goods such as computers
- Save up for expensive items
- Know your overdraft limit and do not exceed it
- Work out a regular budget plan to cover your regular income and expenditure – and stick to it (see Chapter 11 for help and advice)

Remember, debt does not just include forms of credit. Any financial commitment you are unable to meet can become a debt. This can include payment of rent, utility bills or tuition fees. Some debts need to be dealt with in specific ways because of the further problems they might cause. They can be divided into three rough categories – priority debts, educational debts and secondary debts.

Priority Debts

So what makes something a 'priority' debt?

EXAMPLES

Rent arrears – can eventually lead to you being evicted (made homeless)

HP agreement arrears (typically for cars) – goods may be repossessed

Non-payment of Council Tax – imprisonment (in extreme cases)

Non-payment of TV licence – court fines

Non-payment of court fines – imprisonment

Non-payment of gas or electricity bill – disconnection

As you can see from the above examples, priority debts involve a fairly serious sanction if they are left unpaid. In many cases the sanction will only be applied once the creditor has exhausted other measures open to them. For example, it is rare nowadays for someone to face imprisonment for a Council Tax debt unless it is a very old debt that the council has not been able to collect having referred it first to a bailiff (not applicable in Scotland) and then to the magistrates' court for a Liability Order which has remained unpaid. The way in which you deal with a priority debt will depend to a large extent on what the debt actually is.

Rent

If you find you are getting behind with your rent, it is vital that you speak to your landlord as soon as possible. If you can show that it is a short-term cash-flow problem, as is often the case for students who receive irregular student loan payments, your landlord may be sympathetic and allow you to pay the rent when you receive your next loan payment. Unfortunately, this does not always work, especially if the landlord is not used to dealing with students.

If you are in halls of residence, your university may well have organised their payment plan for halls fees to fit in with the payment of student loans, but this is not always the case.

If you do not pay halls fees, your university may do any of the following:

- Issue reminder letters for unpaid rent
- Issue a 'Notice to Quit' bringing your licence (as that is what you will probably have) to an end and giving a date by which you should have moved out
- Refer your case to debt collectors
- Issue court proceedings for recovery of the debt

Ultimately, they may obtain a County Court judgement against you for the debt. This will make it difficult for you to gain access to further credit facilities, or possibly a tenancy through a letting agent, for up to six years. (More on this in Chapter 13.)

In addition, they may also:

- Block your access to library or computing facilities
- Prevent you from progressing to the next academic stage of your course
- Withhold exam results
- Not allow you to graduate if you are in the final year of your course

There are questions as to whether they can actually impose these 'academic penalties' for what is a non-academic debt. If this happens to you, you should contact your students' union immediately.

In the private sector, it depends largely on whether you have a licence or a tenancy. In the case of a licence, non-payment of rent is likely to result in your possessions being thrown out on the street in black bin bags as you have very little protection. The landlord could also take action against you through the Small Claims Procedure. If you have a tenancy, the situation is different.

If you are renting in the private sector and have an 'assured shorthold tenancy', which is the standard tenancy agreement, the law sets out the procedures a landlord must follow if they want to evict a tenant for non-payment of rent. If you have missed only one payment, it is unlikely that the landlord will be able to get you out of the property immediately. In most circumstances, you would need to have missed two payments if you pay the rent monthly, or eight payments if you pay weekly. The landlord must have served a valid Notice of

Seeking Possession and obtained an Order for Possession from the County Court. This obviously does take a while but the bad news is that if it does go to court, the judge has no discretion – if the landlord can show that you owed two months', or eight weeks', rent, both at the time the notice was served and at the date of the court hearing, the judge must order possession. In this worst-case scenario, you would be made homeless and still have to pay the rent arrears, plus court costs and perhaps interest and solicitor's fees.

Even if you do not have two months or eight weeks of rent arrears but are behind or persistently late in paying rent, your landlord may be able to serve notice and get a court order for possession. In these cases, possession is not automatic as the landlord must show that it is 'reasonable' to have you evicted from the property for non-payment of rent. If this happens to you, seek urgent advice from your students' union, student advisers or a local Citizens' Advice Bureau, independent advice centre or law centre.

Council Tax

Remember, not all students will have to pay Council Tax – see Chapter 10 for more information. Make sure that you have given a Council Tax Exemption Certificate, issued by your university, to your local council so they know you are a full-time student. If you are liable to pay, perhaps because you are studying part-time or you live with people who are not students, it is a good idea to pay the tax monthly. Most councils require payment over 10 months, between April and January. If you do get behind on payments, councils vary in their collection procedures, but as a general rule, most will require payment of the bill during that financial year. For example, for a bill issued for 2003/04, the council will require payment by 31 March 2004 at the absolute latest. However, some councils will issue a reminder notice as soon as a payment is missed. This will usually mean that you lose the right to pay in instalments and the entire year's bill is therefore payable immediately. Failure to pay can lead to letters from bailiffs employed by the local council to recover goods equal to the value of the debt owed, and take them for sale at auction. Remember, you do not have to let the bailiffs in if they knock on your door as they are required to gain 'peaceful entry' into the property in order to repossess goods. If you do receive notice of a visit from bailiffs, make sure that the property is secure and all windows are closed so that they cannot get in. If they enter the property once without forcing entry, they can re-enter on subsequent occasions and can use 'reasonable force' to gain entry.

As a last resort, the council may apply to the magistrates' court for a 'liability order', and you could potentially be subject to committal proceedings. This means that you could eventually be sent to prison for non-payment of Council Tax and still be liable to pay the debt on release. Whatever method of recovery the council decides to use, it is very important that you do not ignore the problem. If you deal with it early, you will prevent it from becoming a serious issue and legal costs being added to your debt. As Council Tax is a priority debt, you will need to negotiate with the council to see what repayments they will accept, depending upon your available income.

Gas and Electricity

If you are late in paying a bill, the company will send a reminder bill, usually red to outline its importance, and they will request payment within a short time, usually seven or fourteen days. If the bill remains unpaid at this stage, they may send further reminder letters and refer the account to their legal department or to an external debt collection agency. The letters will take on a more and more urgent tone until you receive a 'Notice Before Legal Proceedings' which may also be called a Default Notice, Final Demand or Notice of Intended Litigation. If you have let it get to this stage, things are now very serious and you may even have your supply disconnected! The notice means that the company will start legal proceedings against you within seven days unless the bill is paid in full. If they obtain a County Court judgement against you, you will then find it difficult to get credit facilities or possibly even tenancies for a period of six years. If you think you may have been overcharged for any period, seek urgent advice from your university's student advisers or students' union.

If you do receive a bill you cannot pay, the first thing to do is contact the supply company to find out if you can pay in instalments.

Bills are often issued on a quarterly basis so they may agree to you paying the bill over the three months as long as it is cleared before the next bill is issued.

Another method used by gas and electricity companies to collect debts is to install a pre-payment meter. These meters are set to collect an amount of the debt each time credit is added to the meter. This means that you cannot run up further debt as you will 'pay as you go' for your gas or electricity and you will slowly clear the outstanding arrears. However, you should remember that these meters will often charge for current consumption at a higher rate and that, if you do not add credit to the meter, you will disconnect your own supply.

One useful tip is to request a monthly budget plan. This is where a monthly payment is taken by direct debit to pay for gas and electricity as you go. This is a very useful way to stop yourself getting into debt with gas and electricity payments. For more on payment methods, see Chapter 10.

Hire Purchase Agreements

Hire purchase, or HP, is where you buy goods and make payments to a finance company who own the goods until you make the final payment. This is quite a common way of buying cars and some household items. If you get into arrears with the repayments, in some circumstances the finance company can repossess the goods without requiring a court order. This is usually the case where less than one-third of the contractual payments have been made and the goods are on 'public ground' as opposed to private property. If you have paid more than one-third of the contractual payments, the finance company will first need to get a court order authorising repossession of the goods, unless you give your consent to the goods being repossessed.

If you are paying for goods on hire purchase and get into difficulty, it might be worth considering a 'voluntary surrender'. This can be particularly useful if you have already paid at least 50% of the purchase price at the time you decide to give up the goods, although you will not get back the money you have already paid. The procedure you need to follow is quite complex so seek advice from a student adviser at your university or students' union if you are considering this course of action.

Educational Debts

'Educational' debts may be either priority or non-priority debts, depending on your individual circumstances.

Student Loan Arrears

If you are still at university but have arrears on a previous student loan for any reason – usually if you have studied previously – you will not be able to get any further student loans or assistance with tuition fees until the arrears are cleared. In this situation, you will probably treat this as a priority debt as it will mean you get no further financial support. There is only one answer here, unfortunately, and that is to pay off the entire amount of the arrears, as required by law. If you find it difficult to raise the money to clear the arrears, you may be able to apply to your university's Hardship, Access to Learning, Financial Contingency or Support Funds for a short-term loan to clear the arrears so that you can continue with your course. For more on these loans, see Chapter 12.

Debts to the University

Procedures vary among universities but it is common procedure for reminder notices to be issued if payments on set dates are missed or if direct debit payments are returned as unpaid by your bank. In some cases, the university will then demand payment of the full out-standing fee in 'cleared funds' (credit or debit card, cash or bank draft) – many will not accept payment by cheque at this stage, especially if a payment has already been returned unpaid. In some cases, if tuition fees remain unpaid, you may have access to information technology or library facilities restricted, and if you have a swipe card that you use to gain access to university buildings, it may be disabled until you have paid your fees.

If fees are outstanding at the end of the academic year, your university may not formally confirm your assessment results to you.

If they refuse to tell you anything about them, you should contact your students' union immediately – such action may breach the Data Protection Act 1998, and you may have rights as a 'data subject' under the Act to have access to all records the university holds about you, including assessment results. If you have not paid the outstanding fees by the start of the next academic year, you may not be allowed to re-enrol for that session until fees have been paid.

If fees are outstanding at the end of your course, your university may withhold formal confirmation of your degree result, although they will probably give you an indication of the result, especially if employment after finishing the course depends on it. You will also probably not be able to attend a graduation ceremony until the outstanding tuition fee debt is cleared.

Ultimately, if you do not clear the outstanding tuition fees, the university will instruct solicitors or debt collectors to pursue the debt through the County Court. You could, therefore, end up with a County Court judgement on your record that will affect your ability to get access to credit facilities for a period of six years.

As with all other debts, the best advice is to deal with the matter early to prevent any further action from being taken. Negotiation with the university finance department at an early stage can sometimes prevent the problem from getting worse. Make sure that your LEA has assessed your fee contribution correctly so that you are not paying more than you need to. Give a copy of the financial assessment to your university so that they know the right amount to invoice you for.

Accommodation Debts

Refer to the section on rent debt, above, for the main provisions for collection of rent arrears and strategies for dealing with the problem.

Non-priority Debts

Non-priority debts include most types of credit, such as:

- Bank overdrafts
- Credit cards
- Unsecured personal loans

- Telephone bills
- Internet bills
- Mobile phone bills
- Cable/satellite television bills

This category can also include educational debts such as tuition fees, especially if you are not due to graduate for some time and have a period in which to raise the money to settle the debt. They are known as non-priority debts because the potential sanctions available to the creditors are much more limited than those available to priority creditors. The main collection options open to a non-priority creditor are to refer the case to a debt collection agency or to issue proceedings in the County Court and secure a judgement against the debtor.

Strategies for dealing with non-priority debts will also differ from those for dealing with priority creditors where individual negotiation with each creditor is very much in order. Here, each non-priority creditor should be treated fairly and equitably.

EXAMPLE

Emily has drawn up her budget and has a monthly surplus, after her essential expenditure, of £25. Emily has applied for all the sources of income she can. She has no priority debts but does have the following non-priority debts:

Eastern Bank Credit Card
Balance £900   Minimum Payment £27
Fabclothes Store Card
Balance £450   Minimum Payment £22.50
Wardrobe Inc. Store Card
Balance £370   Minimum Payment £11.10

As you can see, the minimum monthly payments Emily is due to make to her cards total £60.60, which is more than her available income. Emily could cut back on her spending in other areas or increase her part-time work hours, but this could be of detriment to her studies. Alternatively, she could write to her creditors and ask them to accept reduced payments, taking into account her available income.

Asking Creditors to Accept Reduced Payments

If you are considering asking non-priority creditors to accept reduced payments, there are a number of steps you need to follow.

Step One

Work out a monthly budget plan, including all your essential income and expenditure. Hopefully, as Emily has, you will end up with a monthly surplus.

Step Two

List your creditors, with the total balance owing on each card or to each creditor, and add up the total balance outstanding. In Emily's case, the total outstanding is £1,720.

Step Three

Work out an 'equitable' pro-rata payment to each creditor by using the following method:

$$\frac{\text{Individual balance}}{\text{Total balance}} \quad x \quad \text{Available income}$$

For example, if Emily is trying to work out her monthly pro-rata payment to the Eastern Bank Credit Card, she would do the following:

$$\frac{£900}{£1,720} \quad x \quad £25 \quad = \quad £13.08$$

Based on an equitable distribution of her available income, Emily would offer Eastern Bank £13.08 per month which, as you can see, is lower than her current contractual minimum payment of £27 per month.

Step Four

Draw up a 'financial statement'. This is a budget plan showing essential income and expenditure along with a list of all the creditors, total balances owing to each of them and the monthly offer of payment.

Step Five

Send a copy of the financial statement to each of the creditors along with a covering letter outlining your circumstances and why you cannot meet the current contractual payments. You should also ask each creditor to freeze all interest and charges being applied to the account. If the debt is to a credit card company, you should also return the card to the card issuer. This demonstrates goodwill on your behalf as it shows the company that you will not be able to keep using the card, thus increasing your debt. Make sure that you keep a copy of the letter and financial statement.

Hopefully, each of the creditors will accept your offer, usually for a period of six months, although different creditors have different policies. If any of the creditors does not accept your offer, or you find you do not have a surplus, seek advice from a student money adviser.

Credit References and 'Blacklisting'

You may have heard people say that they cannot open student bank accounts or get access to other credit facilities because they are 'blacklisted'. These people may, in the past, have got into difficulties with repayments on credit cards or personal loans and may have been subject to recovery procedures by the company concerned. If they had not complied with the terms of their contractual agreement – made the minimum monthly payments due on a credit card, for example – then the company may have registered that with a 'credit reference agency'. That record will remain on the person's credit file for a period of up to six years.

What is a 'Credit Reference Agency'?

A credit reference agency is a company that collects information from subscribing companies on how consumers run their credit accounts. Typically, this will include details of the credit limit, whether or not repayments have been made on time and when there are arrears. They may hold information about accounts that have been closed within the last six years, as well as accounts you currently hold. This information will be available to other banks, credit card companies or letting agents who pay to use the services of the credit reference agency. In addition, they will hold certain public record information about you which includes:

- Voters' roll information – this is very important to creditors to whom you might be applying for credit facilities as it helps them confirm that you actually live where you say you live, and how long you have lived there.
- Record of County Court judgements – if a County Court judgement for money is entered against you from a County Court in England, Wales or Northern Ireland, or a Decree issued by a Small Claims and Summary Sheriff Court in Scotland, this will remain on the credit record for six years.
- Bankruptcies and administration orders – details of these also remain on the file for six years.
- Record of searches – the file will also show a list of all the companies who have made a search of your credit file.

It is important to realise that this is all *information* about you – not an opinion and certainly not a 'blacklist', as most people seem to think. When, for example, a bank searches your file, the credit reference agency will supply the information they hold about you to the bank concerned who then apply their own policies in deciding whether or not to grant you access to credit. This is often known as 'credit scoring', and if you reach a certain score you may be granted credit.

How Do I Find Out What Information is Held About Me?

It is estimated that information is held on at least 80% of the adult population of the United Kingdom. The Data Protection Act gives you certain rights. If a company is going to make a search of your credit file as part of the process of dealing with an application, they must tell you. This is so that you can find out exactly what information is held. There are two main credit reference agencies that hold information on consumers in the UK:

Experian Limited
Consumer Help Service
PO Box 8000
Nottingham
NG1 5GX

Equifax plc
Credit File Advice Service
PO Box 3001
Glasgow
G81 2DT

If you are refused credit by any organisation, they must tell you which of the credit reference agencies they have used, if they used an agency when dealing with your application. To find out what information they hold about you:

- Write a letter to the agency, stating that you are writing under section 7 of the Data Protection Act 1998 and you want them to send you a copy of the file that contains information that can affect your financial standing.
- Include your full name and current address and a list of all the addresses you have lived at for the past six years.
- Enclose a cheque or postal order for £2, payable to the credit reference agency concerned.

Send the letter to the agency and make sure you keep a copy. The credit reference agency must reply to your letter within seven working days.

When you receive the file from the credit reference agency, it will contain a variety of codes depending on how your accounts have been conducted. You will also be sent a guide telling you what the various codes actually mean as the different agencies use different codes. Your file may also include the details of other people who:

- Have a very similar name to you and live at the same address
- Are other members of your family living in your household
- In the past have lived with you at your current or previous address

Credit reference agencies must not supply information about anyone else but they may supply the names of other people, whether or not they have a financial connection with you, if they have been listed on the voters' roll at the same address as you.

Correcting Information

If information held about you is factually correct, there is absolutely nothing you can do about it. However, mistakes do happen and if this is the case, you have a right to ask for the file to be corrected.

If the file contains information about other people with whom you have no financial connection, you can ask the credit reference agency to 'disassociate' you so that their information does not appear on your file and vice versa. To do this, write to the credit reference agency concerned and ask them to create a 'disassociation' between you and explain the reason. This could be, for example, a person with a similar name (a family member, perhaps) who has left home and no longer has any financial connection with you. The agency concerned must reply within a certain time to confirm that they have corrected the file. If they do not do this, then the matter should be referred to the Office of the Information Commissioner which has responsibility for data protection and freedom of information issues as this action may be a breach of the Data Protection Act by the credit reference agency. If this does happen to you, seek advice from a student adviser at your university or students' union.

If there is information in the file that is incorrect for another reason, such as a default that has not been recorded as settled or paid, then you can ask the credit reference agency to correct the file. Once again, you will need to write to them, explaining the circumstances and the fact that the debt is now satisfied or settled. It is helpful to enclose confirmation from the company concerned that the debt has been settled. The credit reference agency then has 28 days to confirm that they have either corrected the file, removed the entry or decided not to act at all.

If they have amended the record, they must send you a copy of the revised record. If they do not reply, or say they have not amended the file, you can send them a 'notice of correction', which they will add to your file so that anyone searching it in future will see it. A notice of correction is a statement of not more than 200 words that sets out concisely and clearly why you believe an entry on your credit file is wrong. This might include clarification on an entry such as a default on your credit record if you were ill and not working and not able to afford the repayments. If the agency considers your notice to be frivolous, scandalous, defamatory or not worthy of publication for any other reason, they can refuse to accept it. In all other cases, they must write to you within 28 days confirming that it has been placed on your file. They must also send details to any company that has searched your file in the last six months. In cases where they want to refuse to accept a notice of correction, the agency must first apply to the Information Commissioner for a ruling. Only if the Commissioner agrees with the agency can they refuse to accept it.

Top Tips – Dealing with Debt

- Do not ignore letters from banks and other creditors – the ostrich approach simply does not work!
- Keep statements from all accounts to help you monitor your spending.
- Draw up a monthly budget plan and stick to it!
- Try to do without expensive credit and store cards, but if you do have them, make sure you keep the spending under control and pay the monthly minimum amount.
- Don't leave 'priority' things like rent, tuition, gas and electricity unpaid so that you can pay a credit-card bill – the credit-card company can wait for their money so you can keep a roof over your head!

Getting Help

The following are good sources of help if you are getting into debt

- Most universities now employ specialist student money advisers – sometimes in the student services department or students' union. Most money advisers can offer help with budget planning and money management and may be able to help you when contacting creditors in times of difficulty.

- Local Citizens' Advice Bureaux and independent advice centres, especially in the larger towns and cities, often have dedicated money advice workers, though bear in mind that they may not be used to dealing with students in the same way as student money advisers employed by universities and students' unions.

- The national helplines listed in Appendix B, such as National Debt Line, Consumer Credit Counselling Service and Student Debt Line, can offer self-help packs and telephone assistance.

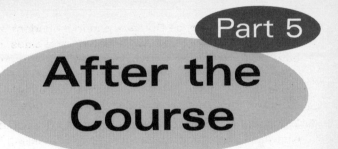

Part 5

After the Course

14

A Glutton for Punishment . . .

Further Study

OK, so you are only just starting out on your first degree, but chances are you may be thinking of postgraduate study. In some cases this will be essential, particularly if you are seeking a career as a solicitor or barrister, architect or accountant, all of which have some postgraduate training requirement. Or you could be studying for a non-teaching degree but plan to go into teaching, so you will need to do a Postgraduate Certificate in Education (PGCE) after you have finished your degree. Whichever situation you are in, you need to think about how you are going to pay for the course before you start.

Postgraduate funding in the UK is very different from undergraduate funding. In most cases, there is no statutory support available – PGCE and architecture diploma courses are the main exceptions – so you will not be able to get a student loan or any of the other funding you would have received as an undergraduate. As a result, you need to look to other sources for funding and start the search early. In some cases, you need to make an application as much as one year before you are due to start the course in order to make sure that funding is in place when you start. Some universities make it a condition of offering a place on a postgraduate course that you have made sufficient provision to support yourself financially for its duration. If you delay your search, you may find you have no way of paying your tuition fees, which are usually higher than undergraduate fees, or of supporting yourself and your family, if you have one. If you remember only one thing, remember to start your search for funding as early as possible, possibly even before you have a confirmed place on a course.

The housing situation for postgraduate students is generally the same as for undergraduates. However, some universities have specific, and sometimes higher quality, accommodation for postgraduates.

This chapter outlines some of the main sources of funding currently available and how and when to apply for them.

Postgraduate Architecture Diplomas

In most cases, the university will have made the offer of a place on the diploma course at the same time as the undergraduate part of the course. It is usually treated as an integral part of the undergraduate degree and therefore tends to be funded in the same way as an undergraduate course.

SEE ALSO
Chapters 2, 3 and 4 on undergraduate funding

Postgraduate Certificate in Education (PGCE)

For funding purposes, the PGCE course is treated as an undergraduate course. Students on this course are therefore entitled to apply to the LEA, ELB or SAAS for support with tuition fees, a student loan and any supplementary grants as outlined in Chapters 2–4 (European Union students should apply to the DfES European Team in Darlington for tuition fee support). Remember, however, that if you are in default on any prior loan with the Student Loans Company, they will not pay your tuition fees or loan. In addition, students on PGCE courses at universities in England who are not already employed as teachers are eligible for a Training Bursary of £6,000 from the Teacher Training

Agency. This bursary is usually available to students from the UK and, unusually for UK student support, the European Union. Arrangements for payment of the bursary vary according to where you are studying, but it will usually be paid in equal monthly instalments. You are, however, advised to check with the university or college that provides the teacher training. You do not need to make an application for the bursary as your university or college will make the arrangements on your behalf.

PGCE students studying a 'shortage subject' at secondary level in England may be able to apply to the university for an award from the Secondary Shortage Subject Scheme. For more information, see Chapter 12. Students can also apply to their university's Hardship, Support or Access to Learning Fund.

If you are training in Wales, the bursary is known as a 'Training Grant' but is administered in the same way as the Training Bursary for trainees in England. If you go on to teach certain subjects – currently maths, science, information technology, design and technology, drama, English or Welsh – at secondary level, you will receive a Teaching Grant of £4,000 after your first successful year of teaching. Applications are dealt with by the Welsh Assembly Government, and you apply during your course of teacher training. You may also qualify for a Secondary Undergraduate Placement Grant of £1,000 if you study one of the above subjects, or £600 if you study another secondary-level subject. The grant is intended to provide support for trainees during periods of school experience and is administered by your university. PGCE students in Wales can also apply to their university for assistance from the Financial Contingency Fund if they are in hardship after starting their course.

In addition, students on PGCE secondary courses may qualify for a Welsh Medium Incentive Supplement of £1,200. This is administered by the university and can be paid to those trainees at secondary level who need extra help in order to eventually be able to teach in Welsh. Entitlement to this grant is not automatic and it is for the university concerned to decide whether or not to make a payment. There is an expectation that when you complete your course you will take up a teaching post in a Welsh-medium school.

Quick Guide – PGCE Funding

- Entitled to student loans, supplementary grants and assistance with tuition fees, subject to means test
- Training Bursary of £6,000 in England – known as a Training Grant in Wales
- £4,000 Teaching Grant for some students in Wales, payable after you have been teaching for one year
- Welsh-medium incentive if you will teach in Welsh
- Secondary Shortage Subject Scheme available in England for trainees studying secondary-level shortage subjects who are in hardship
- Able to apply for Hardship or Access to Learning Funds in the same way as undergraduates

Loans for Postgraduate Study

Instead of student loans, the Government operates a scheme known as the Career Development Loan (CDL) in conjunction with some of the high-street banks – currently Barclays, Royal Bank of Scotland, Co-operative and Clydesdale. To be eligible to apply for a CDL, you must be aged over 18 and plan to work in the UK or a European Economic Area country. Your course should be vocational. A CDL can cover up to 80% of the cost of tuition fees and if the course is full-time, provide some support for your living costs. If you have been unemployed for at least three months before starting the course, a CDL can cover all tuition fees. The minimum amount you can borrow is £300 and the maximum is £8,000. Your course must normally last no longer than two years, or three years if it includes a work experience element. Whilst you are studying, the interest that accrues on the loan is paid on your behalf by the Government and you do not have to make any repayments. You will usually start making payments one month after your course is due to end, at which point you will also be responsible for paying the interest that accrues on the loan.

The banks do run a credit check on all CDL applications and their lending criteria will be applied to the request. Even if you are turned down when you first apply, it is worth trying one of the other banks that operate the scheme as different banks will have different lending policies.

Information on Career Development Loans can be obtained from your university's student services department or the Career Development Loan Helpline on freephone 0800 585 505. Other contact details can be found in Appendix A.

Other banks offer loans similar to CDLs – they may call them 'graduate loans' or 'professional studies loans'. These are not part of the Government scheme but are commercial loans offered by the banks. In some cases, especially with graduate loans, you may be expected to start making repayments as early as one month after taking out the loan. In other cases, the loan will work almost the same as a CDL. If you already have an account with a bank that does not participate in the CDL scheme, it could be worth asking what facilities they can offer you.

Quick Guide – Postgraduate Loans

- Operated by the banks
- Usually credit checked and subject to the bank's lending policies
- A CDL can cover up to 80% of tuition fees and provide some support for living costs
- The minimum CDL is £300, the maximum is £8,000
- CDL Helpline: 0800 585 505
- Other banks offer similar loans – it is worth shopping around

Sponsorship

If you are in employment and considering postgraduate study, it could be worth approaching your employer to see if they are willing to provide sponsorship, for either fees or living costs. Many employers are willing to do this for current employees, whether the course be full-time or a part-time 'day release' course, especially if it is directly related to the job being done and considered relevant for career-development purposes.

Studentships and Graduate Assistants

Some universities offer studentships or allow postgraduate students to work as Graduate Teaching Assistants. A 'studentship' may be in the form of a grant paid by the university towards your living costs, or payment of your tuition fees. Graduate Teaching Assistants may be either paid (at an hourly rate) or receive credits against their tuition fees. It is always worth contacting the postgraduate office of the university you plan to attend to see what is available there. University websites also provide an excellent source of information.

Educational Trusts and Charities

Some educational trusts and charities may be willing to offer support for postgraduate study, but awards are likely to be small and they are quite hard to get. Remember, many trusts receive far more applications than they can provide assistance with, so your application really needs to stand out from the rest to be in with a chance. Some boards of trustees meet only once or twice a year, so with this source of funding it is especially important to begin your search in the academic year before you plan to start your course. Details of trusts and charities can be found in many public libraries. It is also worth looking on the internet as there are now a number of sites that contain contact details for various charitable trusts. You can find a list of some of them in Appendix A. The Educational Grants Advisory Service is also an invaluable resource – their contact details can also be found in Appendix A.

SEE ALSO
Chapter 6 – funding from non-statutory sources

Working Whilst Studying

Working whilst undertaking postgraduate study is another possibility, particularly if the course is part-time or does not involve lots of lectures or laboratory work. It is not advisable, however, to rely on income from part-time work as the sole source of funding your postgraduate study, unless you are studying on a day release or secondment basis.

Benefits and Tax Credits

Students in the vulnerable groups may qualify for benefits. Students responsible for at least one child may qualify for Child Tax Credit, and if you or your partner work at least 16 hours per week, you may also qualify for Working Tax Credit.

SEE ALSO
Chapter 6 – other funding from statutory sources

Disabled Students' Allowances

Postgraduate students can apply for Disabled Students' Allowances (DSA), which can cover the costs of specialist equipment, non-medical personal helpers such as note-takers and other expenditure incurred as a result of being a student. The DSA is available to both full-time and part-time postgraduate students but you need to check that your course qualifies for a DSA – your LEA, ELB or the SAAS will be able to tell you this (they also deal with applications). There is no age limit and the award is not means-tested. If your course is with the Open University, you apply direct to them. The disability officer or adviser at your university will be able to give you more information.

Postgraduate Student Allowance Scheme (Scotland)

The Student Awards Agency for Scotland makes a very limited number of awards to postgraduate students under this scheme. They are mainly available to students studying vocational courses at diploma level or in certain subjects. For further information, contact the SAAS or visit their website at www.saas.gov.uk

European Social Fund (ESF)

Some courses may attract a number of ESF-supported places for certain students, though they will be very limited. Contact the course administrator to find out if there are any ESF-supported places available.

The British Council

The British Council administers a number of awards for international postgraduate students who wish to study in the UK. You should contact the British Council office in your home country for further information of what is available.

Research Councils

These include the following organisations:

- Arts and Humanities Research Board
- Biotechnology and Biological Sciences Research Council
- Economic and Social Research Council
- Engineering and Physical Sciences Research Council
- Medical Research Council
- Natural Environment Research Council
- Particle Physics and Astronomy Research Council

In addition, the General Social Care Council offers some funding to students on postgraduate social work-related courses.

Competition for funding from these councils is very strong and normally only available to students with a first or upper second class degree. Applications should be made to the relevant university department as the councils 'approve' certain research and advanced taught programmes. The university will select applications it thinks are likely to succeed and put them forward to the relevant research council.

Quick Guide – Postgraduate Funding

- Apply early – as much as one full year before you start your course
- Don't put all your eggs in one basket and apply only for a Career Development Loan – if your application is rejected, you will have no money!
- Apply to as many sources as possible and get a good mix of funding that is enough to cover your tuition fees, materials costs and living expenses

15 Repaying Your Loan

One question asked by many prospective and new students is how they are going to repay their loans. Regardless of where you studied or which country of the UK provided your support, there is just one system of student loan repayment.

Under the current rules, you begin repaying your loan in the April after you graduate or leave the course. So if you start a three-year degree course in September 2003 and graduate in the summer of 2006, your loan repayments would start the following April. However, if you start a course in September 2003 and leave the course in January 2004, then your payments would start in April 2004. The Inland Revenue collects payments on behalf of the Student Loans Company for most students. The amount you pay, and even whether you actually make payments, depend on your income, which is why the loans are known as 'income-contingent repayment' loans. The total amount you repay is, in real terms, the same as the amount you borrowed, including a Hardship Loan if you have one of these in 2003/04. The rate of interest is equal to the rate of inflation and is set on 1 September each year. That rate will then apply for the full year. Until September 2003, the interest rate is 1.3% per annum.

Income-contingent Loans – How Do They Work?

The idea is really quite simple. The more you earn, the more you are liable to repay. Under current rules, repayments will only commence if you earn more than £10,000 in a year (tax year from April to April, not an academic year). From April 2005, this will increase to £15,000. Monthly and weekly equivalents are as follows:

Income Level	Monthly Equivalent	Weekly Equivalent
£10,000 per annum	£833.33	£192.31
£15,000 per annum	£1,250.00	£288.46

So, if you earn less than £10,000 in any one tax year (£15,000 from April 2005), you will pay nothing. If your earnings are above that level, your repayment rate is 9% of the excess income. This is best explained with an example:

EXAMPLE

Sameera finishes her course in January 2004. Her repayments are therefore due to start in April 2004. She starts a job soon after leaving university and earns £1,400 per month or £16,800 per year. She is due to start paying her loan once her income reaches £10,000. Her income is £6,800 above this so her repayments are therefore:

£6,800 x 9% = £612 per year, or £51 per month.

Sameera doesn't need to do anything as she is an employee paying tax through the PAYE (pay as you earn) scheme. Her repayments will be automatically deducted from her salary by her employer.

If Sameera's income in any month, assuming she is paid monthly, were to increase, her loan payment that month would increase as well. If she earned less in any month, her loan repayment would decrease. As a result, if she earned nothing at all in any one month then no loan payment would be due for that month. The amounts deducted by the employer will be recorded on the payslips that Sameera receives and also on the P60 she will receive at the end of the tax year. The Student Loans Company will issue an annual statement, showing the outstanding balance at the beginning of the tax year, payments made, interest charged and a closing balance. It is important to note that this information is only passed to the Student Loans Company by the Inland Revenue at the end of the tax year. It is therefore vital that you keep your payslips and P60 in case you need to refer to them at a later date. The P60 is an important document that you may need in order to fill in a tax return, so you should keep this safe anyway – your employer will not be able to give you a replacement if you lose your copy.

Repayments for the Self-employed

Self-employed people do not pay tax to the Inland Revenue in the same way as employees. Instead, income tax is paid through a system known as 'self-assessment'. Rather than loan repayments being deducted at source by an employer, a self-employed person makes a declaration to the Inland Revenue each year on their self-assessment tax return. Total income must be declared and any loan repayment due must be made to the Inland Revenue by the end of January in the following tax year in order to avoid a penalty being incurred.

EXAMPLE

Robert runs his own business. His income for the latest tax year (2002/2003) is £22,000. Under current rules, his income is above £10,000 so he must make loan repayments on £12,000 of his income.

£12,000 x 9% = £1,080.

Robert must, therefore, make a payment of £1,080 to the Inland Revenue no later than 31 January 2004.

Some people may work for an employer and also be self-employed. In this case, employers will deduct loan repayments from income above £10,000 (£15,000 after April 2005) as above. The self-employed person will then need to calculate the amount of repayment due on the total income, i.e. from employment and self-employment, and pay the difference to the Inland Revenue.

Working Abroad

If you work abroad, or for some other reason do not pay tax to the Inland Revenue, loan repayments will be made direct to the Student Loans Company. They will look at your income and calculate the amount you are due to repay. Like all other borrowers, you will start loan repayments in the April after graduation or completing your course, and only if your income is above £10,000 per year (£15,000 after April 2005). There are financial penalties for borrowers who do not supply the Student Loans Company with details of their income or who default on payments.

Finding Out How Much You Owe

You will be sent an annual statement by the Student Loans Company, showing balance at the start of the year, payments made, interest charged and a closing end-of-year balance. This will be issued after the Inland Revenue have sent their notification to the SLC. They will also be able to give you an estimate of when you are likely to finish repaying your loan if you contact them and provide certain information about your current income and repayments made. It is therefore important to keep your payslips.

Regardless of the way in which the loan is repaid, if there is any amount outstanding when you reach the age of 65, the loan will be cancelled, meaning that you will not have to make any more repayments. If your income has never gone above the repayment threshold when you reach this age, you will never have to make any loan repayments. The loan will also be cancelled if you die or become permanently disabled. Nobody else will be made liable for the repayments.

The Repayment of Teachers' Loans Scheme

At present, this is a pilot scheme operating for certain people who enter the teaching profession during 2003/04 or 2004/05. The rules are quite complex and can be found on the internet at www.teachernet.gov. uk. If you qualify for the scheme, the Government repays your student loan for you for as long as you remain teaching one of the qualifying subjects.

Quick Guide – Student Loan Repayment

- You do not have to make any repayments until your income reaches £10,000 per year, or £15,000 after April 2005.
- Repayments are deducted at source by employers. Self-employed people repay through the self-assessment tax system.
- Under current rules you repay 9% of your income that is above the threshold.
- The loan is cancelled when you reach the age of 65 or you die or become permanently disabled.

Glossary

Assembly Learning Grant A grant paid to students from Wales whose families have a low income.

Department for Education and Skills The Government department responsible for student support in England and Wales.

Department for Employment and Learning The Government department responsible for student support for students from Northern Ireland.

Department for Work and Pensions The Government department responsible for benefits in Great Britain (excluding Northern Ireland).

Department of Social Development The Northern Ireland equivalent of the Department for Work and Pensions.

Dependants' Allowances Additional grants paid to students with children or other adults who are financially dependent upon them. Allowances vary across the country so check in the relevant chapter.

Disabled Students' Allowances Special additional grants paid to students with qualifying disabilities. These grants are not means-tested but are based on an assessment of your specific needs.

Education and Library Board The local authority that students from Northern Ireland apply to for student support.

Eligibility Assessment For most students, this is the first stage of an application for student support.

Fee Waiver A means-tested grant, administered by universities, for part-time students on a low income. The grant is used to pay the tuition fees. This is being replaced after the 2003/04 academic year with a Fee Grant, administered by the LEA.

Financial Assessment The second stage of the student support application process for students from England, Wales and Northern Ireland. You need to provide details of your family's income to enable the LEA or ELB to conduct the full assessment.

Hardship Funds These are funds made available to universities by the Government to assist students who suffer financial hardship whilst they are studying. Depending on where you study they may be known as Hardship Funds, Support Funds, Financial Contingency Funds, Access to Learning Funds or Learner Support Funds. The fund is discretionary which means that you are not guaranteed a payment.

Higher Education Bursary A means-tested bursary for Northern Irish students from low income families. The bursary replaces part of the student loan.

Local Education Authority The local authority that students from England and Wales apply to for student support.

NHS Bursary Students on healthcare courses receive bursaries rather than the 'standard' package of student loans.

Opportunity Bursary A bursary available to students from England whose families have a low income. The student must be aged 20 or under on 1 September 2003 and be the first from the family to enter Higher Education. Opportunity Bursaries will be replaced in 2004 with a new Higher Education Grant with no restriction on age.

Ordinary Residence You must be 'ordinarily resident' to qualify for student support. This means that you must normally live in the UK by choice although some temporary or occasional absences are allowed.

Settled Status You must have settled status in addition to ordinary residence to qualify for student support. This means that you must intend to remain in the UK and have no restriction on your stay for an immigration reason. If you are a British citizen or have Indefinite Leave to Remain/Enter (ILR or ILE) you will have settled status.

Social Work Bursary A bursary introduced from September 2003 for students on social work degree courses at universities and colleges in England. The bursary is not means-tested and provides a maintenance grant for living costs.

Student Awards Agency for Scotland The Agency responsible for student support for students from Scotland and for students who will be studying healthcare courses in Scotland.

Student Loan The main source of living costs support for most students. Part of it is means-tested so the amount you can receive will depend on your family's income as well as where you will be studying. Healthcare students can receive non-means-tested loans in addition to their bursaries.

Tuition Fees Since 1998, all students have been liable to make an annual contribution to tuition fees. In 2003/04 the maximum fee is £1,125 but if your family has a low income you may not have to pay the full amount. Scottish students and students from other EU countries who study in Scotland do not have to pay tuition fees.

Young Students' Bursary A bursary paid to Scottish students who study in Scotland whose families have a low income. The bursary replaces part of the student loan.

Young Students' Outside Scotland Bursary A bursary paid to Scottish students who study in England, Wales or Northern Ireland and whose families have a low income. The bursary is paid on top of the student loan.

Appendix A

Government Websites and Helplines

These sites include general information about statutory student support in the United Kingdom.

England and Wales: The Department for Education and Skills
www.dfes.gov.uk/studentsupport
Student Support Helpline: 0800 731 9133
(Contact this number for copies of DfES Guides)

Scotland: The Student Awards Agency for Scotland
www.saas.gov.uk

Northern Ireland: The Department for Employment and Learning
www.delni.gov.uk

You may also find the following websites useful:

Welsh Assembly Government Learning Website
www.learning.wales.gov.uk

Department for Work and Pensions
(Benefits including Income Support, Jobseekers' Allowance and disability benefits)
www.dwp.gov.uk

Department for Social Development
(Northern Ireland equivalent of DWP)
www.dsdni.gov.uk

Inland Revenue
(Responsible for general taxation issues)
www.inlandrevenue.gov.uk

The dedicated Tax Credits site can be found at www.inlandrevenue.gov.uk/taxcredits
Telephone number for Tax Credits forms: 0800 500 222

Helpline: 0845 300 3900 (England, Wales and Scotland)
0845 300 3909 (Minicom: England, Wales and Scotland)
0845 603 2000 (Northern Ireland)
0845 607 6078 (Minicom: Northern Ireland)
Helpline is open 8am–8pm, 7 days per week (excluding Christmas Day, New Year's Day and Easter Day)

Department of Health
(This page contains information about the department's financial support for healthcare students scheme)
www.doh.gov.uk/hcsmain.htm

Useful Contacts

National Government Agencies

Student Loans Company
100 Bothwell Street
GLASGOW G2 7JD
Tel: 0800 405010
(Freephone)
Minicom: 0800 0853 950
(Freephone)
Web: www.slc.co.uk

Teacher Training Agency
(Responsible for funding of postgraduate teacher training courses)
Portland House
Stag Place
LONDON SW1E 5TT
Tel: 020 7925 3700
(general enquiries)
Web: www.canteach.gov.uk

General Social Care Council
(Responsible for social work bursaries in England)
Goldings House
2 Hay's Lane
LONDON SE1 2HB
Tel: 020 7397 5800
(general enquiries: 10am–12pm, 2pm–4pm, Mon–Fri)
Email: info@gscc.org.uk
Web: www.gscc.org.uk

Local Student Support Contacts

This section lists addresses, contact numbers and websites of Local Education Authorities and Education and Library Boards throughout the United Kingdom. Remember, it is the LEA or ELB that you need to contact in order to apply for student support funding, so all you need to do is find your local one from the list and contact them for more information or the relevant forms. If you will be doing a nursing, midwifery or similar health-profession course (not including medicine itself), look under the Healthcare Course Funding.

WARNING!

Local Education Authorities are in a constant process of updating telephone numbers or addresses. This list was correct at the time of writing but may have changed by the time you read this.

Also, some local authorities' student support sections are only open for certain parts of the day (usually but not always the afternoons) at busy times of the year.

a) Local Education Authorities in England

Listed alphabetically

Barking and Dagenham (London Borough)
Education Department
Town Hall
Broadway
BARKING
Essex IG11 7LU
Tel: 020 8227 3309
Fax: 020 8594 9837
Web: www.barking-dagenham.gov.uk

Barnet (London Borough)
Student Support Office
Fenella
Babington Road
Hendon
LONDON NW4 4BS
Tel: 020 8359 2233
Fax: 020 8359 2273
Web: www.barnet.gov.uk

Barnsley
Berneslai Close
BARNSLEY
South Yorkshire S70 2HS
Tel: 01226 773595
Fax: 01226 394011
Web: www.barnsley.gov.uk

Bath and North East Somerset
PO Box 25
Riverside
Temple Street
Keynsham
BRISTOL BS31 1DN
Tel: 01225 394319
Fax: 01225 394011
Web: www.bathnes.gov.uk

Bedfordshire
County Hall
Cauldwell Street
BEDFORD MK42 9AP
Tel: 01234 228149
Fax: 01234 408010
Web: www.bedfordshire.gov.uk

Bexley (London Borough)
Hill View
Hill View Drive
WELLING
Kent DA16 3RY
Tel: 020 8303 7777
Ext 4435
Fax: 020 8319 4302
Web: www.bexley.gov.uk

Birmingham
Council House Extension
Margaret Street
BIRMINGHAM B3 3BU
Tel: 0121 303 3647
Fax: 0121 303 1318
Web: www.birmingham.gov.uk

Blackburn with Darwen
Town Hall
King William Street
BLACKBURN
Lancs. BB1 7DY
Tel: 01254 585192
Fax: 01254 698388
Web: www.blackburn.gov.uk

Blackpool
Progress House
Clifton Road
BLACKPOOL FY4 4US
Tel: 01253 476555
Fax: 01253 476504
Web: www.blackpool.gov.uk

Bolton
3rd Floor Paderborn House
Civic Centre
BOLTON
Lancs. BL1 1JW
Tel: 01204 332140
Fax: 01204 365492
Web: www.bolton.gov.uk

Bournemouth
Dorset House
20–22 Christchurch Road
BOURNEMOUTH BH1 3NL
Tel: 01202 456224
Fax: 01202 456105
Web: www.bournemouth.gov.uk

Bracknell Forest
Student Support Team
Edward Elgar House
Skimpedhill Lane
BRACKNELL
Berks. RG12 1LY
Tel: 01344 354026
Fax: 01344 354001
Web: www.bracknell-forest.gov.uk

Bradford
9 Charles Street
BRADFORD
BD1 1DT
Tel: 01274 752639
Fax: 01274 754843
Web: www.bradford.gov.uk

Brent (London Borough)
Chesterfield House
9 Park Lane
WEMBLEY
Middx. HA9 7RW
Tel: 020 8937 3030
Fax: 020 8397 3040
Web: www.brent.gov.uk

Brighton and Hove
King's House
Grand Avenue
HOVE
East Sussex BN3 2SU
Tel: 01273 293603
Fax: 01273 293456
Web: www.brighton-hove.gov.uk

Bristol City
PO Box 1111
The Council House
College Green
BRISTOL BS99 7EB
Tel: 0117 903 3666
Fax: 0117 903 7800
Web: www.bristol-city.gov.uk

**Bromley
(London Borough)**
Civic Centre
Stockwell Close
BROMLEY BR1 3UH
Tel: 020 8313 4144
Fax: 020 8313 4049
Web: www.bromley.gov.uk

Buckinghamshire
County Hall
Walton Street
AYLESBURY
Bucks. HP20 1UZ
Tel: 01296 383268
Fax: 01296 383367
Web: www.buckscc.gov.uk

Bury
Athenaeum House
Market Street
BURY
Lancs. BL9 0BN
Tel: 0161 253 5000
Fax: 0161 253 5653
Web: www.bury.gov.uk

Calderdale
Northgate House
Northgate
HALIFAX
West Yorks. HX1 1UN
Tel: 01422 392522
Fax: 01422 392515
Web: www.calderdale.gov.uk

Cambridgeshire
Box No ELH 1112
Castle Court
Shire Hall
Castle Hill
CAMBRIDGE CB3 0AP
Tel: 01223 717674
Fax: 01223 717771
Web: www.cambridgeshire.gov.uk

**Camden
(London Borough)**
Crowndale Centre
218–220 Eversholt Street
LONDON NW1 1BD
Tel: 020 7974 1678
Fax: 020 7911 1536
Web: www.camden.gov.uk

Cheshire
Student Support Office
Goldsmith House
CHESTER CH1 1SE
Tel: 01244 603840
Fax: 01244 602304
Web: www.cheshire.gov.uk

**City of London
(London Borough)**
Corporation of London
PO Box 270
Guildhall
LONDON EC2P 2EJ
Tel: 020 7606 3030
Fax: 020 7332 1621
Web: www.cityoflondon.gov.uk

Cornwall
Camel Building
County Hall
Treyew Road
TRURO TR1 3AY
Tel: 01872 322431
Fax: 01872 323839
Web: www.cornwall.gov.uk

Coventry
New Council Offices
Earl Street
COVENTRY CV1 5RS
Tel: 024 7683 1547
Fax: 024 7683 1620
Web: www.coventry.gov.uk

**Croydon (London
Borough)**
Taberner House
Park Lane
CROYDON CR9 3JS
Tel: 020 8760 5768
Ext 2979
Fax: 020 8760 5514
Web: www.croydon.gov.uk

Cumbria
Education Offices
Cumbria County Council
5 Portland Square
CARLISLE CA1 1PU
Tel: 01228 606776
Fax: 01228 606896
Web: www.cumbria.gov.uk

Darlington
Town Hall
DARLINGTON DL1 5QT
Tel: 01325 388809
Fax: 01325 382032
Web: www.darlington.gov.uk

Derby City
Middleton House
27 St Mary's Gate
DERBY DE1 3NN
Tel: 01332 293111
Fax: 01332 716870
Web: www.derby.gov.uk

Derbyshire
County Hall
MATLOCK
Derbyshire DE4 3AG
Tel: 01629 585350
Fax: 01629 585401
Web: www.derbyshire.gov.uk

Devon
County Hall
EXETER EX2 4QG
Tel: 01392 382966 (if you
are from Central Devon)
Tel: 01392 386805 (if you
are from South Devon)
Tel: 01271 388555 (if you
are from North Devon)
Fax: 01392 382203
Web: www.devon.gov.uk

Doncaster
PO Box 266
The Council House
DONCASTER
South Yorks. DN1 3AD
Tel: 01302 737113
Fax: 01302 737223
Web: www.doncaster.gov.uk

Dorset
County Hall
Colliton Park
DORCHESTER
Dorset DT1 1XJ
Tel: 01305 224368
Fax: 01305 224499
Web: www.dorset-cc.gov.uk

Dudley
Westox House
1 Trinity Road
DUDLEY
West Midlands DY1 1JB
Tel: 01384 818181
Fax: 01384 814216
Web: www.dudley.gov.uk

Durham
County Hall
DURHAM DH1 5UJ
Tel: 0191 386 4168
Fax: 0191 386 0487
Web: www.durham.gov.uk

Ealing
(London Borough)
5th Floor
Perceval House
14–16 Uxbridge Road
Ealing
LONDON W5 2HL
Tel: 020 8579 2424
Fax: 020 8758 8881
Web: www.ealing.gov.uk

East Riding of
Yorkshire
County Hall
BEVERLEY HU17 9BA
Tel: 01482 392118
Fax: 01482 884290
Web: www.eastriding.gov.uk

East Sussex
PO Box 4
County Hall
St Anne's Crescent
LEWES BN4 1SG
Tel: 01273 481000
Fax: 01273 481261
Web: www.eastsussexcc.
gov.uk

Enfield
(London Borough)
PO Box 56
Civic Centre
Silver Street
ENFIELD EN1 3XQ
Tel: 020 8379 5366
Fax: 020 8982 7375
Web: www.enfield.gov.uk

Essex
Student & Pupil Financial
Support Service
PO Box 5287
County Hall
CHELMSFORD
Essex CM1 1LT
Tel: 01245 245900
Ext 5902
Fax: 01245 436002
Web: www.essexcc.gov.uk

Gateshead
Civic Centre
Regent Street
GATESHEAD
Tyne and Wear NE8 1HH
Tel: 0191 433 2741
Fax: 0191 490 1168
Web: www.gateshead.gov.uk

Gloucestershire
Shire Hall
GLOUCESTER GL1 2TP
Tel: 01452 425403
Fax: 01452 425399
Web: www.gloscc.gov.uk

Greenwich
(London Borough)
8th Floor
Riverside House
Woolwich High Street
Woolwich
LONDON SE18 6DZ
Tel: 020 8921 8288
Fax: 020 8921 8108
Web: www.greenwich.
gov.uk

Hackney
(London Borough)
Hackney Technology &
Learning Centre
1 Reading Lane
Hackney
LONDON E8 1GQ
Tel: 020 8356 7238
Fax: 020 8356 7235
Web: www.hackney.gov.uk

Halton
Grosvenor House
Halton Lea
RUNCORN
Cheshire WA7 2ED
Tel: 0151 424 2061
Fax: 0151 471 7321
Web: www.halton.gov.uk

Hammersmith
and Fulham
(London Borough)
Student Awards
Town Hall
King Street
Hammersmith
LONDON W6 9JU
Tel: 020 8748 2662
Fax: 020 8576 5686
Web: www.lbhf.gov.uk

Hampshire
The Castle
WINCHESTER
Hants SO23 8UT
Tel: 01962 846434
Fax: 01962 877462
Web: www.hants.gov.uk

Haringey
(London Borough)
Student Awards
48 Station Road
Wood Green
LONDON N22 4TY
Tel: 020 8489 1923
Fax: 020 8862 2906
Web: www.haringey.gov.uk

Harrow (London Borough)
PO Box 22
Civic Centre
HARROW
Middlesex HA1 2UW
Tel: 020 8863 5611
Fax: 020 8427 0810
Web: www.harrow.gov.uk

Hartlepool
Civic Centre
Victoria Road
HARTLEPOOL
Cleveland TS24 8AY
Tel: 01642 523770
Fax: 01642 523777
Web: www.hartlepool.gov.uk

Havering (London Borough)
Student Support Section
The Broxhill Centre
Broxhill Road
ROMFORD RM4 1XN
Tel: 01708 433870
Fax: 01708 433850
Web: www.havering.gov.uk

Herefordshire
PO Box 73
WORCESTER WR5 2YA
Tel: 01905 765904
Web: www.herefordshire.gov.uk

Hertfordshire
County Hall
HERTFORD SG13 8DF
Tel: 01992 471500
Fax: 01992 588596
Web: www.hertscc.gov.uk

Hillingdon (London Borough)
Civic Centre
High Street
UXBRIDGE
Middlesex UB8 1UW
Tel: 01895 250111
Fax: 01895 250582
Web: www.hillingdon.gov.uk

Hounslow (London Borough)
Civic Centre
Lampton Road
HOUNSLOW
Middlesex TW3 4DN
Tel: 020 8583 2811
Fax: 020 8862 5249
Web: www.hounslow.gov.uk

Isle of Wight
County Hall
NEWPORT
Isle of Wight PO30 1UD
Tel: 01983 823486
Fax: 01983 826099
Web: www.iwight.gov.uk

Isles of Scilly
Town Hall
ST MARY'S
Isles of Scilly TR21 0LW
Tel: 01720 422537
Fax: 01720 422202
No website

Islington (London Borough)
Education Department
Laycock Street
Islington
LONDON N1 8DT
Tel: 020 7527 5700
Fax: 020 7527 5565
Web: www.islington.gov.uk

Kensington and Chelsea (Royal London Borough)
Town Hall
Hornton Street
LONDON W8 7NX
Tel: 020 7361 3328
Fax: 020 7361 3481
Web: www.rbkc.gov.uk

Kent
Awards Group
Bishops Terrace
MAIDSTONE
Kent ME14 1AF
Tel: 01622 696570
Web: www.kent.gov.uk

Kingston upon Hull
Essex House
Manor Street
KINGSTON UPON HULL
HU1 1YD
Tel: 01482 613163
Fax: 01482 613675
Web: www.hullcc.gov.uk

Kingston upon Thames (Royal London Borough)
Guildhall 2
KINGSTON UPON THAMES
Surrey KT1 1EU
Tel: 020 8547 4617
Fax: 020 8547 5296
Web: www.kingston.gov.uk

Kirklees
Student Awards Section
Upperhead Row
HUDDERSFIELD HD1 2JL
Tel: 01484 225000
Fax: 01484 225264
Web: www.kirkleesmc.gov.uk

Knowsley
Huyton Hey Road
HUYTON
Merseyside L36 5YH
Tel: 0151 443 3258
Fax: 0151 449 3852
Web: www.knowsley.gov.uk

Lambeth (London Borough)
International House
Canterbury Crescent
LONDON SW9 7QE
Tel: 020 7926 9474
Fax: 020 7926 9397
Web: www.lambeth.gov.uk

Lancashire
PO Box 61
County Hall
PRESTON PR1 8RJ
Tel: 01772 261657
Fax: 01772 261630
Web: www.lancashire.gov.uk

Leeds
1st Floor West
Merrion House
110 Merrion Centre
LEEDS LS2 8DT
Tel: 0113 247 5326
Fax: 0113 395 0219
Web: www.leeds.gov.uk

Leicester City
Welford House
Welford Place
LEICESTER LE1 6ZH
Tel: 0116 252 7855
Fax: 0116 233 9922
Web: www.leicester.gov.uk

Leicestershire
County Hall
Glenfield
LEICESTER LE3 8RF
Tel: 0116 265 6376
Fax: 0116 265 6634
Web: www.leics.gov.uk

**Lewisham
(London Borough)**
3rd Floor
Laurence House
1 Catford Road
LONDON SE6 4SW
Tel: 020 8314 6223
Fax: 020 8314 3019
Web: www.lewisham.gov.uk

Lincolnshire
PO Box 244
LINCOLN LN1 1WN
Tel: 01522 553301
Fax: 01522 553257
Web: www.lincolnshire.gov.uk

Liverpool
Student Awards
Municipal Buildings
Dale Street
LIVERPOOL L69 2DH
Tel: 0151 233 3006
Fax: 0151 233 3029
Web: www.liverpool.gov.uk

Luton
Unity House
111 Stuart Street
LUTON LU1 5NP
Tel: 01582 548080
Fax: 01582 548454
Web: www.luton.gov.uk

Manchester
Awards Section
Education Offices
Crown Square
MANCHESTER M60 3BB
Tel: 0161 234 7078
Fax: 0161 234 7007
Web: www.manchester.
gov.uk

Medway
Student support for students
from Medway is dealt with by
Kent

**Merton
(London Borough)**
Merton Civic Centre
London Road
MORDEN
Surrey SM4 5DX
Tel: 020 8545 3255
Fax: 020 8545 3443
Web: www.merton.gov.uk

Middlesbrough
PO Box 69
First Floor
Vancouver House
Gurney Street
MIDDLESBROUGH TS1 1EL
Tel: 01642 264941
Fax: 01642 264175
Web: www.middlesbrough.
gov.uk

Milton Keynes
Student support for students
from Milton Keynes is
dealt with by
Buckinghamshire

Newcastle upon Tyne
Student Support
Civic Centre
NEWCASTLE UPON TYNE
NE1 8PU
Tel: 0191 232 8520
Ext 25323
Fax: 0191 211 4983
Web: www.newcastle.gov.uk

**Newham
(London Borough)**
4th Floor Broadway House
322 High Street
Stratford
LONDON E15 1AJ
Tel: 020 8557 8668
Fax: 020 8503 0014
Web: www.newham.gov.uk

Norfolk
County Hall
Martineau Lane
NORWICH NR1 2DL
Tel: 01603 222339
Fax: 01603 222119
Web: www.norfolk.gov.uk

North Lincolnshire
Student Awards Team
PO Box 35
Hewson House
Station Road
BRIGG DN20 8XJ
Tel: 01724 297286
Fax: 01724 297242
Web: www.northlincs.gov.uk

**North East
Lincolnshire**
Student Services
39 Heneage Road
GRIMSBY DN32 9ES
Tel: 01472 323323
Fax: 01472 323020
Web: www.nelincs.gov.uk

North Somerset
PO Box 51
Town Hall
WESTON SUPER MARE
BS23 1ZZ
Tel: 01275 884078
Fax: 01275 888834
Web: www.n-somerset.gov.uk

North Tyneside
Student Support
Pametrada Building
Davy Bank
WALLSEND NE28 6UZ
Tel: 0191 200 7070
Fax: 0191 200 5060
Web: www.northtyneside.
gov.uk

North Yorkshire
County Hall
NORTHALLERTON DL7 8AE
Tel: 01609 780780
Fax: 01609 780098
Web: www.northyorks.gov.uk

Northamptonshire
PO Box 216
John Dryden House
8–10 The Lakes
NORTHAMPTON NN4 7DD
Tel: 01604 236290
Fax: 01604 236188
Web: www.northants-ecl.
gov.uk

Northumberland
County Hall
MORPETH
Northumberland NE61 2EF
Tel: 01670 533088
Fax: 01670 533731
Web: www.northumberland.
gov.uk

Nottingham City
PO Box 7167
NOTTINGHAM NG1 4WD
Tel: 0115 915 4994
Fax: 0115 915 4044
Web: www.nottinghamcity.
gov.uk

Nottinghamshire
County Hall
West Bridgford
NOTTINGHAM NG2 7QP
Tel: 0115 977 2277
Fax: 0115 977 2437
Web: www.nottscc.gov.uk

Oldham
Oldham Education Shop &
Advice Centre
5 Regent Chambers
Barn Street
OLDHAM OL1 1LP
Tel: 0161 628 5388
Fax: 0161 911 3221
Web: www.oldham.gov.uk

Oxfordshire
Macclesfield House
New Road
OXFORD OX1 1NA
Tel: 01865 815433
Fax: 01865 791637
Web: education.oxfordshire.
gov.uk/support

Peterborough
Student Awards Service
2nd Floor Bayard Place
Broadway
PETERBOROUGH PE1 1FB
Tel: 01733 748350
Fax: 01733 748333
Web: www.peterborough.
gov.uk

Plymouth
Student Support Team
Civic Centre
Armada Way
PLYMOUTH PL1 2AA
Tel: 01752 253290
Fax: 01752 307403
Web: www.plymouth.gov.uk

Poole
Student Awards
PO Box 722
Civic Centre
POOLE
Dorset BH15 2YE
Tel: 01202 633633
Fax: 01202 633706
Web: www.poole.gov.uk

Portsmouth
Civic Offices
Guildhall Square
PORTSMOUTH PO1 2QU
Tel: 023 9284 1324

Fax: 023 9271 1427
Web: www.portsmouth.gov.uk

Reading
Student Support
Civic Centre
READING RG1 7TD
Tel: 0118 939 0900
Fax: 0118 958 9770
Web: www.reading.gov.uk

**Redbridge
(London Borough)**
Student Awards
22–26 Clements Road
ILFORD
Essex IG1 1BD
Tel: 020 8708 4189
Fax: 020 8708 4193
Web: www.redbridge.gov.uk

**Redcar and
Cleveland**
PO Box 83
Council Offices
Kirkleatham Street
REDCAR TS10 1YA
Tel: 01642 444118
Fax: 01642 444122
Web: www.redcar-cleveland.
gov.uk

**Richmond upon
Thames
(London Borough)**
Student Awards
Floor 1 Regal House
London Road
TWICKENHAM TW1 3QB
Tel: 020 8891 1411
Fax: 020 8891 7714
Web: www.richmond.gov.uk

Rochdale
Student Awards
PO Box 70
Municipal Offices
Smith Street
ROCHDALE OL16 1YD
Tel: 01706 865125
Fax: 01706 658560
Web: www.rochdale.gov.uk

Rotherham
Norfolk House
Walker Place
ROTHERHAM S65 1AS
Tel: 01709 822500
Fax: 01709 372056
Web: www.rotherham.gov.uk

Rutland
Student support for students
from Rutland is dealt with by
Leicestershire

Salford
Minerva House
Pendlebury Road
Swinton
MANCHESTER M27 4EQ
Tel: 0161 778 0123
Fax: 0161 728 6134
Web: www.salford.gov.uk

Sandwell
Student Support Section
PO Box 41
Shaftesbury House
402 High Street
WEST BROMWICH B70 9LT
Tel: 0121 525 7366
Fax: 0121 569 8330
Web: www.lea.sandwell.gov.uk

Sefton
Town Hall
Oriel Road
BOOTLE L20 7AE
Tel: 0151 934 3256
Fax: 0151 934 3239
Web: www.sefton.gov.uk

Sheffield City
Student Support Service
Howden House
1 Union Street
SHEFFIELD S1 2FH
Tel: 0114 273 5635
Fax: 0114 273 5775
Web: www.sheffield.gov.uk

Shropshire
Student Awards
Shirehall
Abbey Foregate
SHREWSBURY SY2 6ND
Tel: 01743 254340
Fax: 01743 254415
Web: www.shropshire-cc.
gov.uk

Slough
Town Hall
Bath Road
SLOUGH SL1 3VQ
Tel: 01753 552288
Fax: 01753 692499
Web: www.slough.gov.uk

Solihull
Student Support Service
Council House
SOLIHULL B91 3QU
Tel: 0121 704 6639
Fax: 0121 704 6669
Web: www.solihull.gov.uk

Somerset
Pupil & Student Services
County Hall
TAUNTON TA1 4DY
Tel: 01823 355455
Fax: 01823 355332
Web: www.somerset.gov.uk

South Gloucestershire
Student Support Team
Bowling Hill
CHIPPING SODBURY
BS37 6JX
Tel: 01454 863292
Fax: 01454 863263
Web: www.southglos.gov.uk

South Tyneside
Student Awards
Town Hall & Civic Offices
Westoe Road
SOUTH SHIELDS
Tyne & Wear NE33 2PL
Tel: 0191 424 7720
Fax: 0191 427 0584
Web: www.s-tyneside-mbc.
gov.uk

Southampton
Student Awards Service
Civic Centre
SOUTHAMPTON SO14 7SA
Tel: 023 8083 3555
Fax: 023 8083 3221
Web: www.southampton.
gov.uk

Southend on Sea
Education Department
PO Box 6
Civic Centre
Victoria Avenue
SOUTHEND ON SEA SS2 6ER
Tel: 01702 215952
Fax: 01702 215000
Web: www.southend.gov.uk

Southwark (London Borough)
Student Support
Education & Lifelong Learning
John Smith House
144–152 Walworth Road
LONDON SE17 1JL
Tel: 020 7525 5214
Fax: 020 7525 5025
Web: www.southwark.gov.uk

St Helens
Student Awards Section
Rivington Centre
Rivington Road
ST HELENS WA10 4ND
Tel: 01744 455329
Fax: 01744 455319
Web: www.sthelens.gov.uk

Staffordshire
Student Support Service
County Buildings
Tipping Street
STAFFORD ST16 2DH
Tel: 01785 278936
Fax: 01785 278639
Web: www.staffordshire.
gov.uk

Stockport
Education Awards
3rd Floor Stopford House
Piccadilly
STOCKPORT SK1 3XE
Tel: 0161 474 3852
Fax: 0161 355 6968
Web: www.stockport.gov.uk

Stockton on Tees
Student Support
Municipal Buildings
Church Road
STOCKTON ON TEES
TS18 1XE
Tel: 01642 393526
Fax: 01642 393479
Web: www.stockton-bc.gov.uk

Stoke on Trent
Student Awards
Swann House
Boothen Road
STOKE ON TRENT ST4 4SY
Tel: 01782 236824
Fax: 01782 236102
Web: www.stoke.gov.uk

Suffolk
St Andrew House
County Hall
St Helens Street
IPSWICH IP4 1LJ
Tel: 01473 584600
Fax: 01473 584624
Web: www.suffolkcc.gov.uk

Sunderland
PO Box 101
Civic Centre
SUNDERLAND SR2 7DN
Tel: 0191 553 1458
Fax: 0191 553 1879
Web: www.sunderland.gov.uk

Surrey
County Hall
Penrhyn Road
KINGSTON UPON THAMES
Surrey KT1 2EX
Tel: 020 8541 9494
Fax: 020 8541 9595
Web: www.surreycc.gov.uk

**Sutton
(London Borough)**
Student Financial Services
The Grove
CARSHALTON
Surrey SM5 3AL
Tel: 020 8770 6640
Fax: 020 8770 6545
Web: www.sutton.gov.uk

Swindon
Sandford House
Sandford Street
SWINDON SN1 1QH
Tel: 01793 463902
Fax: 01793 488597
Web: www.swindon.gov.uk

Tameside
Student Awards Section
Council Offices
Wellington Road
ASHTON UNDER LYNE
OL6 6DL
Tel: 0161 342 2203
Fax: 0161 342 3260
Web: www.tameside.gov.uk

Telford and Wrekin
Student support for students
from Telford and Wrekin is
dealt with by **Shropshire**

Thurrock
Student Awards
Civic Offices
New Road
GRAYS
Essex RM17 6SL
Tel: 01375 652882
Fax: 01375 652792
Web: www.thurrock.gov.uk

Torbay
Student Services
Oldway Mansion
PAIGNTON
Devon TQ3 2TD
Tel: 01803 201201
Fax: 01803 208225
Web: www.torbay.gov.uk

**Tower Hamlets
(London Borough)**
Student Services
3rd Floor Mulberry Place
5 Clove Crescent
LONDON E14 2BG
Tel: 020 7364 4410
Fax: 020 7364 4296
Web: www.towerhamlets.
gov.uk

Trafford
Trafford Town Hall
Talbot Road
STRETFORD M32 0YT
Tel: 0161 912 3234
Fax: 0161 912 3075
Web: www.trafford.gov.uk

Wakefield
Pupil & Student Support
Group
County Hall
WAKEFIELD WF1 2QL
Tel: 01924 305586
Fax: 01924 305632
Web: www.wakefield.gov.uk

Walsall
Civic Centre
Darwall Street
WALSALL WS1 1DQ
Tel: 01922 652379
Fax: 01922 722322
Web: www.walsall.gov.uk

**Waltham Forest
(London Borough)**
Leyton Municipal Offices
Ruckholt Road Entrance
Leyton
LONDON E10 5QJ
Tel: 020 8539 4767
Fax: 020 8496 4558
Web: www.lbwf.gov.uk

**Wandsworth
(London Borough)**
Town Hall
Wandsworth High Street
LONDON SW18 2PU
Tel: 020 8871 8073
Fax: 020 8871 8011
Web: www.wandsworth.gov.uk

Warrington
New Town House
Buttermarket Street
WARRINGTON WA1 2NJ
Tel: 01925 442993
Fax: 01925 442969
Web: www.warrington.gov.uk

Warwickshire
Student Services
22 Northgate Street
WARWICK CV34 4SR
Tel: 01926 418144
Fax: 01926 412746
Web: www.warwickshire.
gov.uk

West Berkshire
Student Awards
Avonbank House
West Street
NEWBURY RG14 1BZ
Tel: 01635 519774
Fax: 01635 519725
Web: www.westberks.gov.uk

West Sussex
Ambassador House
Crane Street
CHICHESTER
West Sussex PO19 1RF
Tel: 01243 777974
Fax: 01243 752170
Web: www.westsussex.gov.uk

**Westminster City
(London Borough)**
Student Support
PO Box 240
City Hall
64 Victoria Street
LONDON SW1E 6QP

Tel: 020 7641 1842
Fax: 020 7641 3406
Web: www.westminster.gov.uk

Wigan
Awards Section
Gateway House
Standishgate
WIGAN WN1 1AE
Tel: 01942 828907
Fax: 01942 828811
Web: www.wiganmbc.gov.uk

Wiltshire
County Hall
Bythesea Road
TROWBRIDGE
Wiltshire BA14 8JN
Tel: 01225 713789
Fax: 01225 713982
Web: www.wiltshire.gov.uk

**Windsor and
Maidenhead**
Student Awards
Town Hall
St Ives
MAIDENHEAD
Berks SL6 1RF
Tel: 01628 796712
Fax: 01628 796408
Web: www.rbwm.gov.uk

Wirral
Student Support Section
Hamilton Building
Conway Street
BIRKENHEAD
Wirral CH41 4FD
Tel: 0151 666 4637
Fax: 0151 666 4338
Web: www.wirral.gov.uk

Wokingham
PO Box 156
Shute End
WOKINGHAM
Berks. RG40 1WN
Tel: 0118 974 6129
Fax: 0118 974 6135
Web: www.wokingham.
gov.uk

Wolverhampton
Student Services
Civic Centre
St Peter's Square
WOLVERHAMPTON WV1 1RR
Tel: 01902 554140
Fax: 01902 554218
Web: www.wolverhampton.
gov.uk

Worcestershire
Awards Section
PO Box 73
WORCESTER WR5 2YA
Tel: 01905 765900
Fax: 01905 765660
Web: www.worcestershire.
gov.uk

York City
Student Support Section
10–12 George Hudson Street
YORK YO1 6ZG
Tel: 01904 613161 Exts.
4251–4255
Fax: 01904 554249
Web: www.york.gov.uk

b) Local Education Authorities in Wales

Blaenau Gwent
Student Support
Victoria House
Victoria Business Park
EBBW VALE NP3 6ER
Tel: 01495 355055
Web: www.blaenau-gwent.
gov.uk

Bridgend
Awards Section
Sunnyside
BRIDGEND CF31 4AR
Tel: 01656 642637
Fax: 01656 668126
Web: www.bridgend.gov.uk

Caerphilly
Student Awards
Caerphilly Road
YSTRAD MYNACH
CF82 7EP
Tel: 01443 864854
Web: www.caerphilly.gov.uk

Cardiff
Pupil & Student Services
County Hall
Atlantic Wharf
CARDIFF CF10 4UW
Tel: 029 2087 2841
Fax: 029 2087 2086
Web: www.cardiff.gov.uk

Carmarthenshire
Student Support
Pibwrlwyd
CARMARTHEN SA31 2NH
Tel: 01267 224502
Web: www.carmarthenshire.
gov.uk

Ceredigion
Education Department
Swyddfa'r Sir
Marine Terrace
ABERYSTWYTH SY23 2DE
Tel: 01970 633662
Web: www.ceredigion.gov.uk

Conwy
Student Support
Government Buildings
Dinerth Road
COLWYN BAY LL28 4UL
Tel: 01492 575051
Fax: 01492 541311
Web: www.conwy.gov.uk

Denbighshire
Student Support
Caledfryn
Smithfield Road
DENBIGH LL16 3RJ
Tel: 01824 706780
Web: www.denbighshire.
gov.uk

Flintshire
Student Support
County Hall
MOLD CH7 6ND
Tel: 01352 704067
Web: www.flintshire.gov.uk

Gwynedd
Student Support
County Offices
CAERNARFON LL55 1SH
Tel: 01286 679162

Fax: 01286 673933
Web: www.gwynedd.gov.uk

**Isle of Anglesey
(Ynys Mon)**
Student Support
Glanhwfa Road
LLANGEFNI
Anglesey LL77 7EY
Tel: 01248 752930
Fax: 01248 752999
Web: www.ynysmon.gov.uk

Merthyr Tydfil
Ty Keir Hardie
Riverside Court
Avenue de Clinchy
MERTHYR CF47 8XD
Tel: 01685 724604
Fax: 01685 722146
Web: www.merthyr.gov.uk

Monmouthshire
Pupil & Student Services
County Hall
CWMBRAN NP44 2XG
Tel: 01633 644510
Fax: 01633 644666
Web: www.monmouthshire.
gov.uk

Neath Port Talbot
Pupil & Student Support
Civic Centre
PORT TALBOT SA13 1RJ
Tel: 01639 763580
Fax: 01639 763444
Web: www.neath-port-talbot.
gov.uk

Newport
Student Support
Civic Centre
NEWPORT NP20 4UR
Tel: 01633 233395
Fax: 01633 244721
Web: www.newport.gov.uk

Pembrokeshire
Student Support
County Hall
HAVERFORDWEST SA61 1TP
Tel: 01437 764551

Fax: 01437 775303
Web: www.pembrokeshire.
gov.uk

Powys
Student Support
County Hall
LLANDRINDOD WELLS
LD51 5LG
Tel: 01537 826000
Web: www.powys.gov.uk

Rhondda Cynon Taff
Student Support
Grawen Street
PORTH CF39 0BU
Tel: 01433 687666
Web: www.rhondda-cynon-
taff.gov.uk

Swansea
Student Support
County Hall
Oystermouth Road
SWANSEA SA1 3SN
Tel: 01792 636000
Web: www.swansea.gov.uk

Torfaen
Student Support
County Hall
CWMBRAN NP44 2WN
Tel: 01633 648121
Web: www.torfaen.gov.uk

Vale of Glamorgan
Student Support
Civic Offices
Holton Road
BARRY CF63 4RU
Tel: 01446 704455
Web: www.valeofglamorgan.
gov.uk

Wrexham
Student Awards & Support
Office
Queens Square Offices
Queens Square
WREXHAM LL13 8AZ
Tel: 01978 297466
Web: www.wrexham.gov.uk

c) Student Support in Scotland

Student support for all students from Scotland is dealt with by the Student Awards Agency for Scotland:

Student Awards Agency for Scotland
Gyleview House
3 Redheughs Rigg
EDINBURGH EH12 9HH

Tel: 0131 476 8212
Fax: 0131 244 5887
Web: www.saas.gov.uk
Email: saas.geu@scotland.gsi.gov.uk

d) Education and Library Boards in Northern Ireland

Belfast
40 Academy Street
BELFAST BT1 2NQ
Tel: 028 9056 4000
Fax: 028 9033 1714
Web: www.belb.org.uk

North Eastern
County Hall
182 Galgorm Road
BALLYMENA
Co. Antrim BT42 1HN
Tel: 028 2565 3333
Web: www.neelb.org.uk

South Eastern
Grahamsbridge Road
BELFAST BT16 0HS
Tel: 028 9056 6200
Fax: 028 9056 6266
Web: www.seelb.org.uk

Southern
3 Charlemont Place
ARMAGH BT61 9AX
Tel: 028 3751 2432
Fax: 028 3751 2490
Web: www.selb.org

Western
Campsie House
1 Hospital Road
OMAGH
Co Tyrone BT79 0AW
Tel: 028 8241 1411
Fax: 028 8241 1400
Web: www.welbni.org

e) Offshore Islands

If you are from one of the following, you should contact the relevant authority for details of their student support schemes as they are different to those operating in the UK.

Guernsey, States of
Student Awards
Grange Road
ST PETER PORT
Guernsey GY1 1RQ
Iel: 01481 710821
Fax: 01481 714475

Isle of Man Government
Student Awards Office
Murray House
Mount Havelock
DOUGLAS
Isle of Man IM1 2SG
Tel: 01624 685790

Jersey, States of
Student Support
Education Dept
PO Box 142
ST HELIER
Jersey JE4 8QJ
Tel: 01534 509500
Fax: 01534 509800

f) European Union Students

EU students studying in England and Wales should contact:

Dept for Education and Skills
EU Students Team
2F – Area B
Mowden Hall
Staindrop Road
DARLINGTON DL3 9BG

Tel: 01325 391199
Web: www.dfes.gov.uk/studentsupport/eustudents/index.shtml
Email: EUTeam@dfes.gsi.gov.uk

EU students studying in Scotland should contact the Student Awards Agency for Scotland at the above address.

EU students studying in Northern Ireland should contact the relevant Education and Library Board.

g) Healthcare Course Funding

If you will be studying nursing, midwifery or an 'allied health profession' (i.e. not medicine or dentistry itself) in **England** contact:

NHS Student Grants Unit (England)
22 Plymouth Road
BLACKPOOL FY3 7JS
Tel: 01253 655655

Tel: 029 2026 1495
Fax: 029 2026 1499

If you plan to study in Scotland, contact the
Student Awards Agency for Scotland.

In **Wales**:
NHS (Wales) Student Awards Unit
2nd Floor
Colate House
101 St Mary's Street
CARDIFF CF10 1DX

In **Northern Ireland:**
If you are from Northern Ireland, contact your Education and Library Board.
If you are from elsewhere, contact the North Eastern Education and Library Board.

Postgraduate Funding

Arts and Humanities Research Board
Postgraduate Awards Division
Whitefriars
Lewins Mead
BRISTOL BS1 2AE
Tel: 0117 987 6543
Web: www.ahrb.ac.uk

Biotechnology and Biological Sciences Research Council
Polaris House
North Star Avenue
SWINDON SN2 1UH
Tel: 01793 413200
Web: www.bbsrc.ac.uk

Economic and Social Research Council
Polaris House
North Star Avenue
SWINDON SN2 1UJ
Tel: 01793 413000
Web: www.esrc.ac.uk

Engineering and Physical Sciences Research Council
Polaris House
North Star Avenue
SWINDON SN2 1ET
Tel: 01793 444000
Web: www.epsrc.ac.uk

Medical Research Council
20 Park Crescent
LONDON W1B 4AL
Tel: 020 7636 5422
Web: www.mrc.ac.uk

Natural Environment Research Council
Polaris House
North Star Avenue
SWINDON SN2 1EU
Tel: 01793 411500
Web: www.nerc.ac.uk

Particle Physics and Astronomy Research Council
Polaris House
North Star Avenue
SWINDON SN2 1SZ
Tel: 01793 442000
Web: www.pparc.ac.uk

Career Development Loans
Tel: 0800 585505
Open 8am–10pm daily
Web: www.lifelonglearning. dfes.gov.uk/cdl

Other Funding Websites

Support For Learning
www.support4learning.org.uk

Scholarship Search UK
www.scholarship-search.org.uk

Funder Finder
Website contains a useful links section to the websites of various charitable and grant-making trusts.
www.funderfinder.org.uk

Educational Grants Advisory Service
www.egas-online.org

Elizabeth Nuffield Educational Fund
A trust that helps students who are single mothers with the costs of childcare.
www.nuffieldfoundation.org/grants/enef/overview.asp

Appendix B

Sources of Further Information and Advice

National Debt Line
Freephone: 0808 808 4000
Open as follows:
Monday and Thursday
10am–10pm
Tuesday and Wednesday
10am–7pm
Friday 10am–12pm

Consumer Credit Counselling Service
Freephone: 0800 138 1111
Open Monday–Friday
9am–5pm
Email: info@cccs.co.uk
Web: www.cccs.co.uk

Student Debt Line
(operated by CCCS)
Freephone: 0800 328 1813
Open Monday–Friday
8am–8pm
Web: www.studentdebtline.
co.uk

Credit Action Student Helpline
Tel: 0800 591084
Open Monday–Friday
8am–8pm

National Union of Students
Nelson Mandela House
461 Holloway Road
LONDON N7 6LJ
Tel: 020 7272 6900
Web: www.nusonline.co.uk

SKILL – The National Bureau for Students with Disabilities
Head Office:
Chapter House
18–20 Crucifix Lane
LONDON SE1 3JW
Tel/Minicom: 020 7450 0620
Fax: 020 7450 0650
Email: skill@skill.org.uk
Web: www.skill.org.uk

Information Service:
Tel: 0800 328 5050
Minicom: 0800 068 2422
Email: info@skill.org.uk

UKCOSA – The Council for International Education
9–17 St Alban's Place
LONDON N1 0NX

Advice line for students: 020
7354 5210
The advice line is open
between 1pm and 4pm
Monday to Friday.
Web: www.ukcosa.org.uk/
pages/advice.htm

Students' Unions in the UK
This website contains an
alphabetical list of UK
students' unions.
www.stu.uea.ac.uk/info/uksu.
html

Citizens' Advice
Online advice:
www.adviceguide.org.uk
To find your local Citizens'
Advice Bureau:
www.citizensadvice.org.uk

National Association of Student Money Advisers
Click on the 'Students' link on
the website for contact details
for money advisers at a
university or college near you.
Web: www.nasma.org.uk

Budget Planner Template

Information on how to complete this template can be found in Chapter 11.

One main tip – make sure all your figures are weekly or monthly. Don't use a mixture as your figures will be misleading and result in a budget you will not be able to stick to. Some of the items listed may not apply to you as this planner is designed to cover as many students as possible – including those with children. You will notice there are also lots of blank lines for you to add your own items as it is not possible to cater for absolutely every income or expenditure source – that would make the planner nearly as long as this whole book!

As a rough guide, the average single person spends approximately £8.00 per week on gas and electricity, and between £25 and £35 per week on housekeeping.

Top Tips!

Useful conversions:

- ANNUAL to MONTHLY – Divide by 12
- ANNUAL to WEEKLY – Divide by 52
- MONTHLY to WEEKLY – Multiply by 12, then divide by 52

Income	£
Student Loan	
NHS or HE Bursaries	
Parent or Partner Contribution	
Wages or Salary	
Dependants' Allowance	
Other Grants	
Scholarships	
Child Benefit	
Tax Credits	
Other Benefit:	
Other Benefit:	
Other Benefit:	
Birthday/ Christmas Money	
Savings	
Trust Funding	

Expenditure	£
Rent or Mortgage	
Service Charges	
Council Tax	
Gas	
Electricity	
Water	
Telephone	
Housekeeping	
Clothing	
Toiletries	
Laundry	
Contents Insurance	
Life Insurance	
TV Licence	
Public Transport	
Car Tax	
Car Insurance	

Income	£
Total Income	

Expenditure	£
MOT and Repairs	
Petrol	
Tuition Fees	
Books and Equipment	
Field Trips	
Lunches at University	
Childcare Costs	
Children's Travel Costs	
Children's School Meals	
Internet Subscriptions	
Clubs and Societies	
Sports Match Fees	
Other Entertainment	
Total Expenditure	

Index

Please note: where an item applies only to students from England, Wales, Scotland or Northern Ireland, this is indicated by E, W, S or NI.